THE
SACRED
CUBICLE

How Workplace Renewal
Begins with You

KIM THOMAS

FOREWORD BY TARA BETH LEACH

The Sacred Cubicle

Trilogy Christian Publishers
A Wholly Owned Subsidiary of Trinity Broadcasting Network
2442 Michelle Drive, Tustin, CA 92780

10 9 8 7 6 5 4 3 2 1
Library of Congress Cataloging-in-Publication Data is available.

ISBN 979-8-89597-242-7
ISBN 979-8-89597-243-4 (eBook)

ENDORSEMENTS

In *The Sacred Cubicle*, Kim pulls back the proverbial curtain between the sacred and secular. Our workplaces are the very spaces God has called us to outwork his mission on this earth. The more we look and act like Jesus, the more our colleagues will see Jesus. Kim shares insightful leadership principles, sage wisdom, and compelling personal stories that not only bridge the gap between faith and work, but help to give meaning and purpose to everything we do.

— Christine Caine
Founder A21 & Propel Women

I come from a large family with southern roots. Financially, we were poor, but we were blessed with a mother rich in wisdom who freely and lovingly shared her strong faith in God.

One of her tenets was to "always do good" and early on in my career, this along with "always take the high road," became my personal mantra. I faced many crossroads when this was not easy to do; however, taking this road always paid off in the end.

Kim has graciously shared virtues to elevate our relationships and work in the business world and in our personal and family life. These virtues are simple yet powerful tools that will always steer us to higher potential to do good.

— Lloyd Dean
Chief Executive Emeritus, CommonSpirit Health

Kim Thomas writes impressively about incorporating the fruits of the Spirit into our "Sacred Cubicles." I appreciate and respect her refusal to shy away from challenging topics, all the while challenging us to embody the Savior we profess to follow, and all the while equipping us by pointing us back to the Spirit. She has written a unique and practical workplace application of Galatians 5:22–23, with strong biblical support from many other places in Scripture. Helpful, compelling read for all of us who want to understand what it means to walk out—and grow—our faith in the workplace.

— Peggy Bodde
Founder of Sacred Work; Author of *Sacred Work:*
A Christian Woman's Guide to Leadership in the Marketplace

The Sacred Cubicle is a powerful guide for Christians seeking to live out their faith authentically in the workplace—a rare and much-needed resource amidst the pressures and fast-paced demands of modern professional life. Through story and practical examples, Kim paints an enriching picture of how to integrate the fruits of the Spirit into their daily work, transforming even the most ordinary tasks into opportunities for spiritual growth. This book is an inspiring call to embrace the sacredness of vocation, reminding us that our work is not just a job, but a divine mission to reflect Christ's love and goodness in every interaction, even in environments where faith is often overlooked.

— Jessica Burton
Director Application Strategy and Lifecycle Management,
Ascension Technologies

The Sacred Cubicle is a must-read for any Christian working in Corporate America. It's so easy to separate our careers from our Christian walk, but Kim uses personal workplace stories to challenge and inspire us to live our faith in the workplace. I feel convicted and encouraged by *The Sacred Cubicle*!

— Liz Chic
Director Tax Credits, Massie R&D

The Sacred Cubicle offers a unique perspective on applying Biblical principles to everyday corporate work. Kim shares her personal experiences living out her Christian faith at work, making it a must-read for professionals seeking to glorify God at work.

— Joe Drygas,
Vice President, State & Local Government, Education & Healthcare, AT&T Business, AT&T

Kim's integration of the Fruits of the Spirit into the workplace represents a profound commitment to partnering with Jesus as we learn to lead from a place deep within our spiritual selves. The chapter on love resonates deeply with me, especially when she states, "I have come to the unshakable belief that love and developing a character of love in our lives and our leadership is the bedrock from which we grow." I highly recommend taking the time to nurture your inner life and outward leadership with Kim's guidance.

— Dr. Kevin Eastway
Author, *Faithful Friendship - Fundraising from the Heart;*
Process Consultant, Design Group International

Kim Thomas details a number of ways to help us perform our work in a manner more consistent with God's character. She does a brilliant job of bringing her day-to-day experiences to the surface in a very relatable way and is authentic about her own learning and growing along her journey. All work is sacred to God, no matter our role and no matter our employer... a church, a Fortune 500 corporation, a small retail outlet, or any other organization. *The Sacred Cubicle* is a wonderful book packed with practical guidance that the reader can apply to grow closer to the Lord and to demonstrate His love in our workplaces.

— Chris Gardner
Senior Pastor, Joyful Life Church;
Customer Success Executive, BMC Software

As someone who has been helping people integrate their faith and work since 2013, I often find that people wrestle with the how. Part of my goal is to help people see that God's Word applies to work as much as it does to other areas of life. In *The Sacred Cubicle*, Kim Thomas does an outstanding job of showing how we can integrate our faith into our work based on the foundation of the fruit of the Spirit. This book is not only packed with practical application, Kim's stories vulnerably and authentically demonstrate what it can look like in real work situations. I highly recommend this book and will be sharing it with those I serve.

— Catherine Gates
Author of *The Confidence Cornerstone: A Woman's Guide to Fearless Leadership*; Executive Director of Polished Network

Kim offers a plethora of situational workplace examples followed by scripture and guides to invite the Holy Spirit to work through us as leaders, offering harmonious solutions for the workplace. This work is a welcome approach, insightful, practical and clearly motivated by the Holy Spirit.

— Jamie Griffith
Founder/CEO, Echelon Search Partners
https://www.cchclonscarchpartncrs.com/

This is a much-needed and inspiring message. *The Sacred Cubicle* has the potential to spark a movement of Christians who see their work as worship and their workplaces as their mission field.

— Tamara Jackson
CEO and Founder of Beaconship

As a local church pastor, I get a front-row seat to the places where faith and work intersect—and at times collide. *The Sacred Cubicle* brings an incredibly relevant perspective, reminding us work isn't just about making a living; it's about living out the way of Jesus right in the middle of the ordinary moments of our jobs. This book is a must read for anyone who is ready to move beyond just showing up on Sunday to actually integrating their faith at work on Monday!"

— Forrest Jenan
Lead Pastor, Neighborhood Church, Visalia

Kim Thomas has an extraordinary ability to deal with the subject of the places of work as a calling and a mission field. This she derives from her experience and work for over 30 years in corporate America. That was often defined by the attitude and behavior of profit first, cutthroat competition, winners and losers and each person for oneself.

In this book, *The Sacred Cubicle*, she highlights the great and boundless potential that corporate has within her sight and grasp of a transformed work environment in which the workplace reflects the goodness of God.

— Dr. Robert Obol Nyeko
Vice President Mission Integration, Mercy Health System

Many of us consider God when we enter a church building, read our Bibles, get married, and raise our children. However, we rarely think about how and what God could heal the world through us in our work and workplaces. Kim Thomas guides us in applying and enjoying the Fruit of the Spirit to our work—a place where we spend a significant portion of our lives and is ripe for transformation. *The Sacred Cubicle* offers a path to sanctify our work and workplaces.

Sean Palmer
Teaching Pastor, Ecclesia Houston;
author *Speaking by the Numbers* and *Unarmed Empire*

The Sacred Cubicle is a powerful guide for integrating faith and work, showing how the fruits of the Spirit can transform our professional lives, and be a visible witness to the beauty of the Kingdom of God. With practical wisdom and deep biblical insight, the book challenges Christians to see the workplace as a sacred space where God's love, grace, and truth can flourish. Whether you're navigating corporate challenges or seeking to live out your calling, this book equips you to embrace your work as sacred and missional. A must-read for anyone serious about integrating faith and work!

— Lisa Rodriguez-Watson
National Director, Missio Alliance

Kim Thomas radiates the love of God. And she does so not because she compartmentalizes her faith or ignores the difficult parts of life, but because she's radically committed to a way of knowing Jesus that embraces and integrates all of life. As a pastor who longs for all people to see their work as ground zero for their formation and participation in God's mission, what Thomas offers us in *The Sacred Cubicle* is an extraordinary gift!

— Rev. Dr. JR Rozko
Pastor for Calling & Community Formation,
Common Life Church;
Co-Founder, Canton Abbey;
Director of Missional Innovation,
Diocese of Churches for the Sake of Others;
Director of Ecclesiastical Advancement,
Order of the Common Life

With enthusiasm and delight, author Kim Thomas invites the reader to a take a fresh view of an ancient idea: work as a holy vocation. She invites us all to see our jobs as much more than means to an end, instead offering a missional understanding of the concept of work. *The Sacred Cubicle* transforms both the drudgery and cutthroat nature of the marketplace into a sacred space, one that's filled with purpose, spiritual formation for our own souls, and a powerful opportunity to share Jesus with our coworkers.

— Aubrey Sampson
Speaker, podcaster, pastor, and bestselling author of *Known*, *The Louder Song*, and *What We Find in the Dark*

Our work is our worship to God by serving His other children. Kim Thomas' book, *The Sacred Cubicle*, provides a transformational road map on how to do that.

— Sam Thevanayagam
President & CEO of Parts Life & Deval Lifecycle Support

The Sacred Cubicle by Kim Thomas is a powerful, practical guide for Christians seeking to live out their faith in the workplace. Drawing from her own experiences in corporate America, Kim dovetails insights on how to navigate professional challenges while being a bold and authentic witness for Christ. This book will inspire you to discover new ways to integrate your faith into your daily work life, leading to greater fulfillment, purpose, and impact in both your career and your personal walk with God.

— Sara Watson
Principal, Capgemini America, Consumer Products,
Retail & Distribution at Capgemini

Core to happiness is loving who you are, what you do, and who you do it with. Kim Thomas does a fantastic job of weaving in meaningful personal stories with practical advice by inviting the principles of Christianity to turn your work from a career to a calling. And the calling into a job you love. A fun, spiritual, quick read that I would highly recommend.

— Laura Young-Shehata
Chief Applications Officer, Ascension Technologies

DEDICATION

For the CommonSpirit Health End User Services (EUS) team members from 2004–2023: You inspired me every single day. It was a great privilege and joy to be your leader; I love you all so much and I will always be *for* you!

CONTENTS

FOREWORD

by Tara Beth Leach

Work—whether we realize it or not—has always been sacred.

From the dawn of creation, work has been woven into the very fabric of God's creation. In the first breath of Genesis, we glimpse a Creator at work, His hands shaping the cosmos, painting the skies to the hues of sunrises and sunsets, molding the earth and cosmos. God crafted beauty out of chaos and poetry out of madness. And in His image, we too were fashioned, called to join Him in this sacred task of cultivating and caring for His creation. In other words, we have been created to work.

Yet, as we step into today's world of fluorescent-lit offices, tight deadlines, and corporate meetings, the word "sacred" can feel distant. The buzzing of emails and boardroom discussions seem far removed from the holiness and wonder of God's original intent. But perhaps, even in these spaces, there's still divine purpose waiting to be discovered.

In *The Sacred Cubicle*, Kim Thomas offers us a profound reimagining of what it means to live and work with sacred intention. Her words are a timely reminder that wherever we are—whether in a corporate office, a classroom, or a construction site—we are still on holy ground. Our cubicles, conference calls, and spreadsheets may not resemble the Edenic garden, but they are still spaces where we participate in God's ongoing mission of renewal and restoration. Kim's book is a much-needed invitation for us to see work not just to an end but as a sacred calling to reflect God's love and goodness right where we are.

In the world of corporate America, we are bombarded by a culture of hustle, success at all costs, and relentless ambition. There's always another goal to reach, another promotion to chase, and it's easy to lose sight of the deeper meaning of our work. But Kim reminds us that work, at its core, was never meant to be about our own glory. It's about joining in God's work of renewal—of participating in the flourishing of others, of embodying kindness, patience, and integrity in environments where those virtues are often in short supply. Kim draws us back to the original purpose of work—to cultivate and steward the gifts we've been given for the sake of God's kingdom.

In my years of pastoral ministry, I have seen firsthand the exhaustion that so many leaders in corporate environments carry. The pressure is overwhelming, the lines between work and personal life often blurred beyond recognition. And in those moments of fatigue and disillusionment, it's easy to wonder, "Does my work even matter? Can I truly make a difference in such a cutthroat environment?" That's why I admire *The Sacred Cubicle* so deeply. Kim Thomas doesn't shy away from the hard realities of corporate life, but she offers a vision of hope. She encourages us to lean into the presence of God in our work, to see our tasks, however mundane or challenging, as opportunities to reflect the love of Christ.

Kim's own journey through the highs and lows of corporate America has given her deep wisdom and insight, which she generously shares in this book. Her words remind us that even in the most difficult workplace environments, we are still called to be faithful. The call to embody Christ doesn't end when we clock in. Instead, it is in the very places where grace, humility, and kindness are most absent that our witness to Christ becomes the most powerful. Every email, every decision, every conversation can become an offering of worship when we choose to engage in our work with God's purpose in mind.

As you read *The Sacred Cubicle*, my hope is that you will find not just practical insights but a renewed sense of purpose in your work. You will be reminded that no matter where you are, God is at work, and He invites you to join Him. Whether you're leading a team, navigating difficult decisions, or managing the everyday tasks that often feel insignificant, know that your work is sacred. It is a place where God's kingdom breaks in, where you get to participate in His story of redemption and renewal.

I'm so thankful for Kim's courage and faithfulness in sharing this message, and I believe her words will be a gift to anyone who reads them. So, as you turn these pages, may you be encouraged, challenged, and inspired to see your work as part of God's sacred mission.

— Tara Beth Leach
Pastor, Good Shepherd Church
Naperville, Illinois

INTRODUCTION

When many think of work, whether it's corporate America, a construction site, or a Hollywood studio, one of the last things they think of is holiness. They think of a culture of cutthroat, profit first, winners and losers, and an every person for themselves mentality. It conjures up images of ruthless interactions, competition, and mind numbingly uniform cubicles. If I am honest, it can feel far from the vibrant life in Christ we long to cultivate as Christians. In my thirty-four-plus years of experience in corporate America, I have, at times, witnessed all of this to be accurate. As such, I have experienced and observed many behaviors, patterns, and attitudes that don't reflect the life of Jesus. This is a challenge and an opportunity for Christians in the workplace. We are called to reflect the goodness of God, and God's goodness isn't cutthroat, dog-eat-dog, or ruthless; instead, it's righteous, honorable, and kind. With such a contrast in behaviors, if Christians walk in step with Jesus, it shouldn't be a challenge to reflect His goodness to our leaders, coworkers, and all who we encounter in our workplace. Approaching our work life with a Christ-like posture will enable us to participate in the mission of God. After all, that is our purpose: the Great Commission that Jesus gives His followers. Let's take a look at some of the instructions Jesus left for us:

"The harvest is great, but the workers are few" (Luke 10:2). Often, when we ponder about the workers being few, the workers most of us tend to think of are church volunteers, missionaries, or pastors. We have been shaped to place the accountability of sharing the gospel on those who hold an official role in the church. I don't think these are the only types of workers Jesus is referring to in this passage. While the seventy-two disciples were sent to "Judea, Samaria, and unto the ends of the earth," we have been sent to conference rooms, department meetings, and unto the limits of Zoom. What an amazing opportunity! If Christians are to follow His command in Matthew 28:19–20, where He says, "Therefore go and make disciples of all nations, baptizing them in the name of the Father and of the Son and of the Holy Spirit, and teaching them to obey everything I have commanded you. And surely I am with you always, to the very end of the age," Then we must realize that we are all sent ones; therefore, each is trusted with the sacred duty of embodying the Good News right where we are. Jesus isn't ambiguous, nor does He place boundaries or caveat these instructions.

In other words, Jesus doesn't say go out and make disciples:

- If you are a man.
- If you have enough money.
- If you are called to be a pastor.
- If you are a Sunday school teacher.
- If you are a carpenter.
- If you are sanctified.

There are no disclaimers in His command; rather, He calls each of us.

- Male or female

- Rich or poor
- Pastor or politician
- Sunday school teacher or college professor
- Carpenter or corporate attorney
- Restaurant owner or waiter

We all received the same set of instructions, meaning we are all sent ones!

Christians in the workplace need to remember that people will look at them and either find Christianity more attractive or less attractive. They will be curious about your faith, or they won't be. Our actions and behaviors drive their curiosity, apathy, or repulsion. How do we, as Christians in the workplace, take our responsibilities seriously and lean into the glorious mission of God?

Being a follower of Christ also compels us to look inward. When I am honest with myself, I know that my actions, behaviors, and certainly my thoughts are not always aligned with the Jesus I know and read about in Scripture. The Jesus that I know and love. And yet, as a Christian, I am called to make every effort to live in a way that demonstrates the love and compassion of Jesus to those around me. Failure to do that is not only my individual disobedience, but our failure to do this collectively as Christians has negatively impacted the perception of Christians, and ultimately Jesus, throughout the world. We, us, you, and me, have participated in actions or behaviors that have hurt the mission of God and have left many wondering how good this God could really be. What an egregious consequence.

I wonder who may have turned from Christianity based on one of my actions. Based on one of my social media comments, or because of a remark I made in a meeting, or because I didn't respond to their text message. I wonder who may have said, "That's the final straw; I've seen enough. I'm done with Christians" because of me, something I did, or something that came out of my mouth. With great opportunity comes great responsibility.

Kara Goldin founded Hint, a healthy lifestyle brand that produces unsweetened water. In a 2019 article in *Forbes* magazine, Kara wrote:

> *One of the founding principles of my business was that I didn't want to use sweeteners or preservatives in our beverages. However, most major retailers require certain products to have a long shelf life, and every industry expert told me that preservatives were the only solution.*
>
> *Though I risked missing out on critical sales opportunities, I refused to compromise my original mission. Instead, I kept pushing suppliers to find a way until we eventually hit on a perfect solution. Today, the products of our mission to make America healthier can be found on the shelves of hundreds of big supermarkets.*
>
> *Your mission should be the ultimate guide for every decision you make about your business. Never forget this purpose, and you'll always retain your integrity.[1]*

Our purpose is clear. We have been invited or, more accurately, commanded to partner with God and other Christians to further the mission of God in this world. If our mission is God's mission, we should frame all our decisions from this lens. No matter how dog-eat-dog a situation might feel or how lost we find ourselves in the sea of gray cubicles, every interaction is an opportunity to refuse to compromise our original mission.

Did you realize that God was the first worker and that work was good? Often, we see work as a means to an end. We have to work to provide shelter, clothing, and food; while that may be true, there is much more to work than toiling. Work had a sacred purpose from the very beginning. In the first chapter of the Bible, we see God at work. In Genesis 1:26–28, God creates humans and commands them to reign and govern over the earth. Work came before the fall of creation, which means work is inherently good.

Pastor Tim Keller wrote extensively on the goodness of work. He said, "The fact that God put work in paradise is startling to us because we often think of work as a necessary evil or even punishment. Yet we do not see work brought into our human story after the fall of Adam, as part of the resulting brokenness and curse; it is part of the blessedness of the garden of God."[2]

In *The Deeply Formed Life*, Pastor Rich Vilodas declares all work as holy. He says:

> *This simple theological conviction that all work is holy*
> *is a necessary correction to a worldview that splits*
> *work into two categories: sacred and secular. According*

to many, the "holy" work is supposed to be exclusively
that which relates to God, the church, missions, or
humanitarian endeavors. And, of course, this work
is holy. But it's not the only holy work. The work of
artists, builders, teachers, parents, entrepreneurs, and
bus drivers is on the same level. We collectively join
to make the world a better place, each of us doing our
part. To see all work as holy is a spiritual practice that
pushes back on a spiritual elitism that obscures God's
good vision for all creation.3

Pastor Vilodas points out that while specific ministry positions are essential to the mission of God, they don't have exclusivity on holy work. Pastors generally don't spend their time in the marketplace—the rest of us do. Those of us that work the nine-to-five, so to speak, or the graveyard shift at a diner. Wherever we are, we can join God at work in making the world a better and more holy place.

So far, we can note three things. We are sent. We are called to mission. And work is good. But then we wonder about the how? Personally, how do I respond as a sent one? How do I partner with God on a mission in this complex world? How do we stay kind when the office jerk makes our lives miserable yet again? How do we remain faithful when we are passed by for the promotion we thought we deserved? There is good news in this! We aren't alone, and God does not send us without skills. Instead, God equips us in many ways, and it all starts with Him giving us the Holy Spirit.

The Holy Spirit, one of three persons in the Trinity, guides us. It is our job to be open to the Spirit. When we actively listen, the work of the Spirit through us will help bring people we encounter to Jesus. In Galatians 5:22–23, Paul describes the fruit of the Spirit. He says, "But the Holy Spirit produces this kind of fruit in our lives: love, joy, peace, patience, kindness, goodness, faithfulness, gentleness, and self-control." When we are walking in the Spirit, we will bear witness to our good God by exhibiting these qualities—even while we are at work.

I once heard Nona Jones, the Chief Content and Partnerships Officer at YouVersion, say, "Our job role and job description is what we get paid to do but being a Christian in our workplaces, that is our assignment." She's right; the assignment God gave us is to be a Christian who is in the world but not of the world. So Christians, as you go about your day in the corporate world or your vocation, remember that your boss may give you a job description that you need to follow or duties to perform, but you have also been given the ultimate assignment to be on a mission with the Triune God in your workplace. Your task is to show those you work with that there is a better way to live this life: to follow Jesus and partner with Him to bring others into the Kingdom of God.

Barna published a study in 2018 on Christians at work.[4] In the study, they identified three types of Christians at work, and they called them vocational personalities.

The compartmentalizers represent 34 percent of Christians, describing these workers as pragmatic but without strong connections to their faith or work.

The second group, the onlookers, represents 38 percent, and these are passive employees who are positioned to better connect with their faith and work.

The third and final group is the integrators. This group represents 28 percent of Christians in the workplace, and Barna describes them as enthusiastic employees who are deeply connected to their faith and work. My friends, this is the group that we want to be a part of.

Integrators see their work as purposeful and a good fit; this pattern holds throughout their responses. Barna had each group respond to the following statements. They noted that the integrator responses were much higher than the compartmentalizers and the onlookers:

- I feel called or made for my current work.
- I am always looking for ways to improve.
- I attend church monthly or more often.
- I strongly believe I have a responsibility to tell others about my faith.
- I strongly agree God gave me certain gifts and talents to use for His glory.
- I strongly agree I want to use my gifts and talents for the good of others.

As a Christian, I completely agree it's important to serve others in my workplace.

I was fortunate to spend most of my corporate career working for an organization grounded in faith and the Catholic tradition. CommonSpirit Health is inspired by 1 Corinthians 12:7, which states, "Now to each one the manifestation of the Spirit is given for the common good." The mission includes making the healing presence of God known in the world. They believe that humanity holds the power to heal, and they take kindness seriously, even trademarking the word humankindness. Wander the halls of the workplace, and you can see signs of humankindness and faith throughout; it can cause one to catch their breath. The history includes seventeen congregations of religious women, and today, CommonSpirit Health carries on their work, which began more than 780 years ago.

Phil Graves, Patagonia's senior director of corporate development, says, "You can be called to be a plumber or a fisherman or a venture capitalist as long as you live your values and faith through what you do—that's what matters. We need more Christians to approach their work this way and not decouple their faith from their vocation."[5]

I often hike in the mountains near my home in Southern California. When I step foot on the trails, I enter a place that feels like a cocoon. I am at peace, and I am in awe of the sheer goodness of God's work, creation. It is sacred. Our workplaces can be like that. Our job may not look like a beautiful craggy mountainside, it may not sound like a cascading stream, it might not smell like the crisp scent of pine needles, but if God's at work, it's just as sacred.

When we abide in God, the fruit of the Holy Spirit pours out of us. In *The Sacred Cubicle*, we will examine the fruit of the Spirit, how the fruit is cultivated in our lives, and ultimately, how we share the Good News of a good God in our places of work. And it doesn't matter where you are working. Because every classroom, every factory, every call center, every grocery store and beyond can be sacred. Every cubicle can be a sacred cubicle.

CHAPTER 1

Joy

Never let anything so fill you with sorrow as to make you forget the joy of the risen Christ.

— Mother Teresa[6]

It had been a tough week, month, year, or several years, for that matter. As a healthcare information technology leader who was entering month eighteen of the COVID-19 pandemic, I was tired. All I could do was put one foot in front of the other and navigate my way from my bedroom to the bathroom in fifteen steps, then to the coffeepot in ten steps, and finally to my home office in thirty more steps. It was Saturday, and I had already worked seventy-five hours that week. It would be another day of staring at my screen on Zoom calls, and I was weary of almost every aspect of my job. I missed life before the pandemic.

The team I led was exhausted. They served on the frontlines in hospitals across the country. Between Covid, forest fire evacuations, and unrelenting projects the people were fatigued. Pre-pandemic, I was one flight away from being right there with them, in the trenches, so to speak. Now, I couldn't travel, and my webcam confined me, while the heavy pressures of my role weighed on me. We were working on a project with unrealistic expectations, and nobody wanted to hear why it wasn't possible. We were all under pressure, and everyone just wanted it done. It was big; we were pulling rabbits out of hats to get as much as possible completed, but we would never meet the expectations. We knew it, and while we continued communicating it, it felt like it didn't matter. I experienced dejection, my team felt discouraged, and while I kept telling them, "Don't worry, I'll handle it," I knew they were all nervous. Even through a computer monitor, I could see it in their eyes, sense it in their voices, and hear it in their words. Despair was in the air, as thick as the smoke from the fires raging throughout the western United States.

The work had reached a fever pitch and COVID-19 had taken its toll. We had lost several team members since the onset of the pandemic, and a longtime employee had just succumbed to cancer. I had watched this employee's kids grow up into teenagers, and now they were without their father. Loss and grief rippled through the teams. When I became a leader, I never thought I would become well-versed in managing employee deaths, but over those two years, I became an expert. In fact, in recent months, others had asked me what to do in these times. When an employee died, other leaders knew that beyond knowing the process, I was available to lend an ear and share advice. I did my best to console team members and even our lost team members' families. Despite being dispersed across the country, our team was so close that I spoke at three memorial services. Our team photos appeared in several celebration of life videos. Our colleagues were dying, and joy was evaporating.

There were other pressures: staffing, sick employees, global supply chain issues, and now vaccine mandates. The COVID-19 vaccine mandates meant some people would be let go, worsening our understaffed situation. Turns out, being part of IT in a clinical environment during a global pandemic is a tough gig. Attrition skyrocketed in healthcare and technology, and we're both. Financial constraints and negative attitudes were prevalent; even minor inconveniences seemed monumental and unmanageable. Every week, I dedicated a significant amount of time to encouraging team members and leaders throughout the organization to persevere, but even I felt discouraged, reaching a point where I could barely offer encouragement to others.

Larry, my right-hand employee and friend for twenty-two years, had expressed his frustration to me. To know Larry is to know perseverance and a can-do attitude, no matter what. The problem had to be bad for Larry to express disillusionment. He explained he was emotionally and physically wiped out. He couldn't continue to work long hours with so little recognition of the hard work the team was doing. It was too much. Larry had long been what we often refer to as a workaholic, and he said to me, "You know, in the past we would work until all hours of the night, but it was fun. I just don't have that fun anymore; now it's a grind." He had decided to look for outside employment for the first time in twenty-six years. I felt crushed, but he was right; it was no longer fun.

I couldn't visualize working without Larry by my side. Larry and I create a near-perfect balance. He is brilliant, and his spreadsheet skills could be an actual superpower. He gets the data, we create the plans, I sell the plans, he takes care of the details, and I lead the team. Imagining work without Larry was too hard to bear. As we talked, I knew we could make tactical changes that would improve his work-life balance, but I didn't know how to get that fun back. When I hung up the phone with Larry, it was at that exact moment that I realized I had lost my joy.

The Joy Gap

MIT conducted a multi-year study on joy in the workplace and discovered what they call "The Joy Gap." In a recent article, they outlined how big the joy gap is. The article published in 2022 said:

> *In our original 2018 Joy@Work study, we found a stark gap between the levels of joy people expected to feel and the joy they actually experienced: Fifty-three percent of survey respondents who said they expected to feel joy at work reported that they did not actually experience it. Because most people spend a majority of their waking hours working, this joy gap has a pernicious effect on our overall joy, happiness, outlook, and well-being. In 2021, we conducted our survey again. In just three years, the joy gap had widened substantially — from 53% to 61%. The pandemic has highlighted what's important, at work and in life: taking care of one another, finding joy even in hardship, and looking for moments of meaning.*[7]

What Is Joy?

Merriam-Webster defines joy as the emotion evoked by well-being, success, or good fortune or by the prospect of possessing what one desires:

1. the expression or exhibition of such emotion
2. a state of happiness or felicity
3. a source or cause of delightful[8]

Joy is a powerful emotion; it's a Fruit of the Spirit. It's mentioned 218 times in the NIV Bible. In Psalm 100, the Psalmist exclaims: "Shout for Joy to the Lord all the earth!"

Many expressions we use mention joy.

- A bundle of joy
- Jump for joy!
- Joy ride
- A thing of beauty is a joy forever
- Pride and joy

As human beings, we crave joy. Don't believe me? Go out to Amazon and do a book search for Joy. I just did, and let me share with you what I found:

- Over 60,000 books about joy
- 202 books about joy coming out soon
- 8 books about joy debuted today!
- 12 books about joy released yesterday

Are you as surprised as I was about the number of upcoming book releases on the topic of joy? As I was browsing through the titles, it became clear to me that people are in search of joy and will look everywhere to find it. Here are a few of the pending releases about Joy:

- *Finding Joy in the Empty Nest*
- *40 Days to a Joy-filled Life*
- *The Joy of Cannabis*
- *The Joy of Science*
- *Laundry Love: Finding Joy in a Common Chore*
- *The Joy of Weeds*
- *The Joys and Disappointments of a German Governess in Imperial Brazil*
- *The Joy of Wanderlust: The World's 100 Most Magical Places*
- *Black Boy Koy*
- *The Joy of Eating*
- *The Joy of Small Things*
- *And Yet: Finding Joy in Lament*
- *The Joy of Pizza*
- *The joy of basketball*
- *The Joy of Photoshop*
- *The Joy of Hearing*
- *A Salad Only the Devil Would Eat: The Joys of Ugly Nature*
- *Mother Trucker: Finding Joy on the Loneliest Road in America*
- *The Joy of Living Clean and Sober*

- *Better Than OK: Finding Joy as a Special Needs Parent*

We are individuals who are looking for joy in countless ways. I am a foodie and enjoy trying new and interesting food. You bet *The Joy of Pizza* attracted me when I read through that book list. I love to travel, so naturally, I gravitated to *The Joy of Wanderlust: The World's 100 Most Magical Places*. The third book that caught my eye was *And Yet: Finding Joy in Lament*. The grief over many things in the last few years of the pandemic has influenced me to look for joy in lament.

As humans look for joy in everything from pizza to the common chore, Christians have a leg up. Our joy shouldn't require a search because it comes from God, through the Spirit, and because we have hope that Jesus gave us through resurrection.

I was definitely in a joy gap. Joy that once flowed out of me had somehow disappeared. I had to ask myself why. Was I too preoccupied to experience joy? Were our challenges so significant that joy seemed inappropriate or disingenuous? Was I just focused on the wrong things? Had I grown so weary of the pandemic that it had taken all the joy out of my work?

While these contribute, when you walk in the Spirit, you can still radiate joy amid deadlines, meetings, unrealistic expectations, and even in a pandemic. It all comes down to the work the Spirit does in us much more than in our circumstances. I'm a Christian, so why was I in a joy gap?

Restoring Joy

Bill Hutterly led a large team of people for me in Arizona and Nevada. Bill is compassionate, emotive, and I often describe him as one of the most genuine people I know. Like me, he loves his team. He lives in a suburb of Phoenix, and when he showed up on my doorstep in Pasadena, California, unannounced, in October 2021, I knew something was wrong. I took one look at his face and asked him, "What's wrong? Are you leaving?" With a quivering lip, he nodded yes, and tears immediately fell from his eyes. We stood in my home office, we hugged, and we cried openly. This was a blow. Like Larry two months before, he said it wasn't fun anymore.

As we talked, I realized that I had let him down on a few things, and I felt disappointed in my leadership. Bill pushed his anger toward Human Resources, but I looked at him and said, "Don't blame HR; this is my fault. I am your leader, and I should have helped you." It was an emotional day. Tears fell more than once as we talked about what we could do to make the situation right. Ultimately, Bill turned down another job and stayed with me, our team, and our company, but the months of extreme difficulty had taken their toll. Something had to change.

I began a period of deep discernment in regard to my role as vice president. What could I do to turn around the state we were operating in? What was in my control? What change could I influence? Over several days, I intentionally prayed over the situation. I asked God to help provide direction for me, and I realized a few things. Instead of focusing on people, I had been focusing on deadlines and every difficulty that was being thrown our way. Relationships and people have always been central to my work. One could say it's my superpower. It's why I do what I do, but I was putting tasks, spreadsheets, and presentations ahead of relationships. I was responding to the crisis of the day rather than pushing back on it or coming up with creative solutions. I had lost my way. Developing people and improving lives, whether it is those who work for me or those around me, has always driven me. However, I had hidden this passion amongst the gray clouds of other priorities. The clouds, the rain, and the windy culture had seemingly caused my joy to vanish. But if joy isn't about external circumstances, I had to ask myself, where had mine gone?

I reflected on why I had lost my joy and what was contributing to this slow leak and my empty bucket. While I knew I had allowed my quiet time to wane, I hadn't realized the impact of it. I had inadvertently done away with my morning routines, which contributed to my joy gap. The Spirit had stopped radiating joy through me because I had stopped walking and abiding every morning with the One who could renew my soul. I had allowed that time to be replaced with COVID-19 conference calls, mind-numbing scrolling, or choosing the snooze button and extra sleep instead of feeding my soul. The Bible reminds us that weeping can stay for the night, but joy comes in the morning. As I pondered, I knew I needed to become more intentional about my morning routine.

As I reflected on my habits, I realized that, as I woke, I allowed morning stress to become my priority. I needed to take these deadlines, pressures, and worries to God instead of holding them myself. Instead of starting my day with emails and calls, I needed to start my day with verses and prayer. I looked at my schedule for opportunities and began making changes. Getting up earlier and adjusting some meetings provided adequate time for contemplative prayer, rest, and solitude instead of moving it to the evening or skipping it altogether. I started prioritizing things differently, talking to my people more rather than spending time on less critical tasks. Finally, I managed to convey to my leader that I needed to be more considerate of my time, resulting in slower responses than what she was used to.

As I began starting my day again by being led by the Spirit, I saw my attitude evolve almost immediately and joy return to my heart. The people I was leading saw the change, too, and they saw it right away. The joy of the Lord was evident. Within a few weeks, my leader said to me, "Can you give me some of whatever you have that rebooted your attitude?" I joked that I had started watching more TikTok, but then I told her what I had actually done. I had placed importance on the wrong things. If we were going to make it through this challenging season of post-COVID-19 and all the pressures that came with it, I had to change my priorities and my routine.

I am not suggesting that reestablishing your morning time with God will suddenly ease all of your work pressures, nor am I saying that things will get simpler. I am suggesting that following God is a daily, moment-by-moment choice, and if you aren't intentionally feeding your soul, you can't possibly be at your best. In Matthew 22:37, Jesus says this:

> *"Love the Lord your God with all of your heart, with all of your soul, with all of your mind, and with all of your strength."*

Loving God with your heart, soul, mind, and strength happens when you are in daily conversation with God. Spending time in God's presence is crucial to our formation and our witness in the workplace. I can't honestly tell you that every time I read the Bible, a surge of joy hits my heart and my cup runneth over, but when I spend time in God's presence, I encounter the closeness of the Spirit; I feel the fruit from that experience, and that includes an abundance of joy. When I am walking throughout my day knowing that I genuinely do love the Lord, my God, with all my heart, soul, mind, and strength, I am a walking testament of love and joy. A sense of tranquility fills my body, enabling me to be more tolerant and understanding towards my children and colleagues. I show more kindness and gentleness; I exhibit more self-control, and all of this wraps up in faithfulness.

So, while my circumstances didn't change when I started my new routine, my approach and attitude did. Changing my morning regimen helped set my day up for success by refocusing me on the priorities at work that were most important to my role. As a leader, I often have competing tasks and demands for my time. My most important job is my responsibility to the people working on my team. It's something I take seriously, and when I didn't take time to recharge my batteries and feed my soul, it was impossible for me to do that well for others.

Having joy or even finding joy once we have lost it doesn't mean we won't have bad days. It doesn't mean that we are free from depression, anxiety, or any other mental health problems. These afflictions are real. I have personally experienced both high anxiety and depression before, and it is a significant drain on our bodies. Fortunately, God provides us with lifelines to help us through these times or these conditions. When we use physicians, medicine, and each other, we can lean into the future when, one day, our bodies, minds, and spirits will be restored to God's ideal for us. A day will come when pain, cancer, loss, and depression will no longer exist, and on that day, we will be made new. But what about now? If you are experiencing anxiety or depression, I encourage you to contact your physician and tell your spouse or a trusted friend. God provides us with people who can help us; we shouldn't be afraid to draw on these resources.

Work Is a Gift from God

Alex Liu has earned a reputation as an expert on joy at work in the business world. In 2022, he published a book called *Joy Works: Empowering Teams in the New Era of Work*. In his book, he describes a Japanese concept called ikigai, which centers on the reason and purpose of work.[9] It's a brilliant book about cultivating joy in the workplace and not settling for anything less. As I read it, it prompted me to think about the reason that we work.

I have heard many say that we work and toil because of the Fall. As I mentioned in the introduction, the Fall occurs in Genesis chapter three, bringing original sin into the world. Original sin disrupted the perfect relationship between God and His people; it brought shame and brokenness into the world. There is no doubt that sin has made our vocations more difficult. Imagine a workplace without shame, arguments, impulsivity, and self-centeredness, and you know that the Fall affected our jobs.

But did you realize God introduced work before the Fall, not afterward? Genesis chapter two, verses 2–3 says, "By the seventh day God had finished the work he had been doing; so on the seventh day he rested from all his work. Then God blessed the seventh day and made it holy, because on it he rested from all the work of creating that he had done." Not only does the Bible start with God doing work, but right away, God introduces Sabbath and rest. A few verses later, God puts Adam to work. Verse 15 says, "The Lord God took the man and put him in the Garden of Eden to work it and take care of it." Adam's next responsibility is naming all the animals. Our work is not punishment or a means to an end; it should be a source of joy because it's a gift from God and one that existed from the beginning.

Happiness

While we know that joyfulness comes from the power of the Spirit, happiness can come from external circumstances. Joy and happiness are different, but they get linked together. Happiness and fun make for a better work experience. Be a happiness cultivator at work; people will want to be around you if you spark happiness rather than misery when someone sees you approach their desk. I had a conversation with a colleague who told me they had been nervous about coming to a team dinner. She said, "I had been so nervous because I didn't know anyone, but the second I approached the table; you were so welcoming, you immediately put me at ease and made my defenses evaporate. It was such a great night." She said that whenever she sees me in the hallways of the office, it puts a smile on her face and joy in her heart. I remembered the dinner. When she approached the table, I stood up, warmly greeted her, and ensured she sat in a central location. Paying just a small bit of extra attention to her ensured she was comfortable.

Barbara Markway writes for *Psychology Today* and gives tips for growing happiness. I found three of her tips to be extremely helpful for the workplace.[10]

The first one is to savor the moment. She tells us to engage all our senses, hold that moment for 15–20 seconds at least, and just savor it. When something good happens, stop, take it in, and enjoy every minute of it.

Another tip is to practice non-judgmental awareness of yourself and others. Barbara states, "Most people, including you, are doing the best they can with the resources they have. No one wakes up and says, 'I think I'll screw up my life today.' Give yourself, and others, a break." Our world is so judgmental. These days, judgment is so normalized that we rarely even realize we are doing it.

A few months ago, one of my girlfriends challenged me to recognize the number of times I used the words, "I'm freaking out." Apparently, I was saying it often. I started paying attention and began stopping myself from repeating this phrase. I have applied this same concept to being judgmental, and I have been surprised by how often and how broadly I internally judge people. Talk about a joy killer; judgment breeds dissatisfaction. When it comes to being judgmental, I encourage you to take a similar challenge, pay attention to your judgmental thoughts, and redirect them. Like me, you may notice that you spend too much thought power on unnecessary and unholy judgment.

Barbara advises us to resolve conflicts proactively. Don't let them fester. When a dispute goes unattended, it can eat away at our happiness and bring us down. Deal with conflict kindly and timely.

Happiness looks different from person to person. Some people couldn't be happier than when they are curled up on the couch reading a book. Sitting at home reading may sound miserable to a person who thrives on dynamic, high-energy interactions. Recognizing and appreciating these individual preferences can transform a workplace. Truly engaging with coworkers, beyond the typical icebreakers or "fun facts," creates a foundation for genuine connection. One of the most fulfilling aspects of my career has been making the effort to know people personally—not just as colleagues, but as individuals with unique lives and interests. This investment builds a culture where people feel valued and seen, fostering a sense of belonging and collective joy.

Celebrations foster joy and happiness. Recognize and celebrate your colleagues! I celebrate work successes on the company's social media and my personal platform. Social media can be tricky, so please make sure you stick to the rules of your organization. Look for creative ways to celebrate people; I downloaded an app on my cell phone called Thnks. This app allows you to send people all kinds of things, from a $5.00 cup of coffee to a $500.00 gift card. It has something unique for every budget. Parties, handwritten cards, phone calls, and even texts can be celebratory. Take the time to recognize those you work with. When we celebrate people, we lift them up. Take every opportunity to lift and encourage those around you.

Create opportunities to help your community. Organize a community service project with your coworkers. I am always proud of our team members when we connect and serve the poor and powerless. Find a couple of non-profits to invest your time in. Nothing quite bonds us together like giving back to the community. Over the years, our teams have routinely set aside days to work at food banks and offer technical support to others in need. Get creative and use the talents of your team to benefit the people in the areas where you live and work. In the past, our IT teams have partnered with financially constrained school districts to prepare computers and donate them to classrooms and training labs. We have also collectively given to our communities through food drives and Christmas gifts for those in need.

A few years ago, the *Huffington Post* analyzed how the average person spends their time. The results might be a little surprising to you. I know they were to me. Over a lifetime, the only activity that beat out work was sleeping! Your highest waking activity is likely work. In fact, the article stated that the average person spends thirteen years and two months of their life at work![11] Considering the time of your life that you spend working, it would be very unfortunate if you spent that time being miserable.

Of course, we all can experience happiness gaps, but if that gap is consistent or you are failing to find happiness in your job, it may mean it is time to move on. As I described earlier, I have been in seasons of happiness gaps, but mostly, I love what I do and where I have worked.

If you are in a toxic work environment, remember that it doesn't own you and certainly doesn't own your joy. It's important to remember that God wants the best for us, and while we know God doesn't call us to a life that is free of suffering, and sometimes that may be our vocation, it's also crucial that we take care of our mental and physical health. If you feel stuck in a toxic environment, I suggest you approach work with open hands, knowing that you may need to find something else. Then submit to prayer, get a discernment group to pray alongside you, consider a business coach, and engage with God as He leads the way.

Tips and Biblical Encouragement

As you reflect on being joyful at work, consider:

1. When you are experiencing trouble, know that your external circumstances do not own your attitude and cannot take away your joy.

    Consider it pure joy, my brothers and sisters, whenever you face trials of many kinds because you know that the testing of your faith produces perseverance.

    — 1 James 1:2–3

2. I know we live in an increasingly virtual world but don't underestimate the value of spending time with people. Face-to-face is even better.

I have much to write to you, but I do not want to use paper and ink. Instead, I hope to visit you and talk with you face to face so that our joy may be complete.

— 2 John 1:12

3. Start your day in the presence of the One who gives you joy.

    For his anger lasts only a moment, but his favor lasts a lifetime; weeping may stay for the night, but rejoicing comes in the morning.

    — Psalms 30:5

4. Start a gratitude journal for work. Mine is simple. It's a Google document where I write something I am thankful for at work once a day. Sometimes, it's a paragraph; other times, it's a word or two, but when I feel happiness waning, I can return to my journal and see nothing but gratitude.

    Rejoice always, pray continually, give thanks in all circumstances; for this is God's will for you in Christ Jesus.

    — 1 Thessalonians 5:16–18

5. Remember you have a purpose, a God-given purpose, and your godly assignment works hand in hand with the job you are paid to do.

Therefore go and make disciples of all nations, baptizing them in the name of the Father and of the Son and of the Holy Spirit.

— Matthew 28:19

6. Don't forget that joy is evident and contagious. When you exhibit joy, people will notice, and it will make them feel good to be around you.

    A cheerful heart is good medicine, but a crushed spirit dries up the bones.

    — Proverbs 17:22

7. God rested, and so should you. There isn't a reward for those who skip their vacation or cannot rest. Sabbath is important, so take time to restore your soul.

    There are six days when you may work, but the seventh day is a day of sabbath rest, a day of sacred assembly. You are not to do any work; wherever you live, it is a sabbath to the LORD.

    — Leviticus 23:3

Reflective Questions

1. Reflect on James 1:2–4, which encourages us to consider it joy when facing trials. In what ways can we

cultivate a spirit of joy, even when we are experiencing
challenging trials?

2.   How does our relationship with God impact our ability
     to experience joy?

3.   How can we, as Christians, support and uplift our
     colleagues who may be struggling with their own "joy
     gap"?

4.   What are some practical ways we can integrate prayer
     and reflection into our daily routines to maintain a
     focus on God's presence?

5.   How can we use our work to demonstrate the joy of
     Jesus to others?

6.   What does it mean to live out the Great Commission
     in your workplace, and how can joy play a role in that
     mission?

7.   Consider Philippians 4:11–13, where Paul speaks about
     learning to be content in all circumstances. How can we
     find joy in the small, everyday moments and cultivate a
     spirit of contentment in our lives?

CHAPTER 2

Peace

Peacemaking is a full-time vocation that includes each member of God's people.

— Henri Nouwen[12]

He banged his fist on the table, and we all froze in fear. It was 2005, and I was a new leader in my first manager job. The HBO show, *The Sopranos*, was at the height of its popularity. If you are unfamiliar with this TV series, it centers on an Italian mob boss named Tony Soprano. People commonly referred to my boss as Tony Soprano. We all knew why; he scared people, and he scared me. It seemed like there was anger and controversy everywhere he went, and he often left a path of destruction in his wake. If he was walking down the hall, it was not unusual to see people turn around and take the longer route to avoid him. He was difficult, hard to please, and often combative. A cloud of fear hung over them, as they dreaded the thought of being fired by him at any moment, for any reason.

Five of us were in this meeting, and when he banged his fist on the table and uttered a few swear words, we were all nervous. Who was going to get the brunt of our leader's anger? As he erupted on the colleague sitting next to me, I felt thankful that it wasn't me, but I felt bad for my teammate. Our boss rarely took out his anger on me, but I was always afraid I would be next. His posture and attitude reflected rage under the surface, and his direct reports lived in a state of fear. Mindy, a coworker and close friend, got to where she could no longer work for him. She left the company; she felt it was her only way out.

During the two years that I worked for my tough leader, everything I did was with great trepidation. As the book by Bessel van der Kolk says, "the body keeps the score." While I didn't receive the brunt of his unacceptable behavior often, I was afraid. Unbeknownst to me, my body noticed before I did. A couple of months into working for him, I began to experience chest pains. They would typically come during downtime, late in the evening when I was at home getting ready for bed, or on the weekend when I was enjoying a chai tea with my mom. I went to the doctor, underwent tests, and several times, my husband and I ended up in the emergency room in the middle of the night. Chest X-rays, lab work, and an EKG would produce nothing wrong. When my chest pains eventually subsided, I began to have strange neurological issues. I would feel as if my brain wasn't operating correctly. In one meeting, I remember turning to a senior executive and asking, "Do I look okay? I feel like there is something wrong with me." After a CT scan showed everything was normal, my symptoms changed yet again.

Next up, abdominal pains, irregular menstrual cycles, and headaches before we circled back to chest pains again. I was thirty-one and had already had a colonoscopy, endoscopy, mammogram, multiple EKGs, and MRIs. Guess what they discovered? Absolutely nothing. I was the epitome of good health. Eventually my doctor said, "Maybe it's just stress?" I didn't believe it. I couldn't fathom these physical ailments being because of stress. Things were great at home, and I loved everything about my job. I didn't feel stressed at all. Nevertheless, she persisted, and ultimately, I was prescribed Xanax with a promise to take it the next time I got chest pains.

Without fail, the chest pains came back. I took the .25 milligrams of Xanax, and the chest pains subsided within twenty minutes. I was stunned. I realized I had been having a panic attack. As I settled into the realization that I had been having panic attacks for two years, I felt blown away. What caused my panic attacks and these strange signs and symptoms? I couldn't figure it out.

Eventually, my colleague Ben and I summoned the courage to speak up about our difficult leader. We realized that even though we were new leaders and others were ignoring the toxicity of the situation, it was our responsibility to ensure we and our teams could work in peace. As a result, some organizational changes were made, and we ended up working for a new director. Oddly enough, within a few months, all of my confusing symptoms disappeared. I realized that for two years, I had been living in a state of high alert, and my body was holding the brunt of it. My heart raced with anxiety, anticipating the moment my unpredictable leader would unleash his wrath upon me, just as he had done to countless others. I was not at peace, which caused stress in my body, mind, and spirit.

If you have spent time in the workforce, you have likely encountered these people who are the antithesis of peacemakers.

You know them. They instigate, gaslight, push people unnecessarily, and often go unchecked.

- It's the person who is more interested in assigning blame than solving the issue.
- It's the leader that loses her temper in meetings.
- It's the employee who gossips about their coworkers and seeks to cause conflict.
- It's the leader who instantly catastrophes problems.
- It's the team member who is quick to criticize others.
- It's the leader who diverts the problem to the employee rather than offering support.
- It's the coworker who is stirring the pot.

Likely as I described these types of people, a name or two popped into your mind, but fortunately, these agitators are in the minority of people we encounter at work.

Peacemaking

While most of us would like to think of ourselves as peacemakers, I don't know that most of us live up to that word. I confess I would not rate myself a ten out of ten on peacemaking at work. I might give myself a seven. I don't generate conflict, and it's not that I don't know how to be a peacemaker. I find I don't always choose to utilize that skill, even though I know how to diffuse most conflicts and bring an out-of-control situation to reconciliation. All too often, I choose to "stay out of it" or say "it's not my problem," or use one of the latest viral phrases, "not my monkeys, not my circus." Too often, I take the simple route by not engaging or discussing my opinion behind the scenes, but not helping to reconcile the situation. I think many of us hang out in the middle and keep watch on both sides, but that is not peacemaking; that is passive, and peacemaking is a verb. Peacemaking requires action.

The entire story of God demonstrates peacemaking, with Jesus as the ultimate peacemaker. When people recognize you using your skills as a peacemaker, they realize there is something different about how you value people, approach conflict, and live your life. Christians, peacemaking is essential, and it requires action on our part.

I recall a three-day meeting I was hosting with my direct reports. During the session, I had a challenging topic I wanted the team to work through. I gave them the subject and instructions and left the conference room so they could dive deep into the situation. About an hour later, I received a text from someone in the room telling me I needed to get back in there. I went back and found the team at complete odds with each other. They weren't seeing eye to eye, and the situation had become quite hostile. I had them take a break and instructed them to go for a walk, get coffee or a snack, rest, and return in thirty minutes. When everyone was back in the room, we sat down and walked through how it became such an emotionally charged situation.

I wish that when the meeting was over, the outcome thrilled everyone, but that wouldn't be true. Peacemaking doesn't guarantee that everyone will get what they want. For starters, some people desire the wrong outcomes. Second, humanity's brokenness means that not everything in the marketplace is a win-win. Our goal is to find solutions that benefit everyone involved, although it may not always be possible.

One of my team members didn't show up that night for the team dinner. The intensity of his anger was so palpable that he couldn't bring himself to sit down and share a meal with us. I know some leaders would have demanded he come to dinner or reprimand him afterward. After all, it wasn't optional, but I didn't believe that would help anyone get to a peaceful place. I gave him space and texted him after dinner, asking if he was available to talk. He said yes, and we met outside the restaurant, which was adjacent to our hotel.

I told him, "You go first," and he unleashed a torrent of emotions, expressing his deep sadness and frustration with the outcome and with his peers. I just held space; I listened. I nodded, not in agreement but in an understanding of his truth. If I was going to bring him toward reconciliation with the team, I needed to show him the respect he didn't show me when he skipped our team dinner. I needed to meet him where he was in his anger, frustration, and hurt. We spent two hours together, and I worked to lean into his view and see things from his perspective. Afterward, I showed him the others' viewpoints, pointed out commonalities, and got to the point of reconciliation. The next day, he came to the meeting with a renewed spirit; he apologized for his words the day before, and others apologized to him for the frustration. The following two days were full of productive conversations, strategic planning, and positive teamwork.

I sought him out for peacemaking. Had I been passive in this situation, not only would it have set the trajectory for conflict throughout the rest of our meeting, but afterward, he would have returned home angry and discouraged. Instead, he returned home knowing that his leader valued his viewpoint, respected him personally, and would go the extra mile to ensure he felt cared for. Whether at home or at work, peacemaking requires action.

I have used these five simple steps in times of peacemaking:

1. Build a foundation of trust by demonstrating understanding and compassion. Be empathetic.
2. Seek common ground.
3. Lean into the other fruit of the Spirit. It would be difficult to be a peacemaker if you weren't showing patience, kindness, or gentleness.
4. Work towards reconciliation.
5. Be honest. Sometimes, we just need to acknowledge that a situation isn't fair. This acknowledgment is an act of seeing the other person.

My friend, Larry Rench, is a film orchestrator in Hollywood. He has been working in the film industry for over thirty-five years. When asked how he shows peacefulness in the workplace, Larry shared this:

> *As I reflected on this question, several stories came to mind of times when composers have let out a sigh of relief when I would walk into the room of a recording studio for a scoring session. More than once, composers have said that they were so happy when I walked into the room because they knew then that everything was*

going to be alright. You see, the scoring session is the culmination of weeks or even months of hard work, where the creation of the music to underscore a movie moves from the synthesizers in a composer's home studio to a recording date filled with musicians ready to sightread and record the music for the soundtrack that will give the film its emotional connection to an audience. It costs a lot of money to hire a whole orchestra of world-class musicians and the stakes couldn't be higher. My job as an orchestrator is to translate the notes from the virtual sounds of a synthesizer to notes on a page that musicians will perform, giving life to the music. It all comes down to this, and there is a lot of tension in the room prior to the first downbeat. It's at that moment, when composers are most vulnerable, that I have heard over and over again that a sense of peace comes over them as I walk into the room. My job is done by that time, but they know I have worked hard behind the scenes to make sure that every note that will be played is correct, that the dynamics and phrasing I have put into the music is right for the part, and that there won't be any mistakes that will have to be corrected when every minute of recording time is costing thousands of dollars. My presence in the recording studio is a reflection of the peace and presence of Christ who has gifted and enabled me to use my talents in this way to help others. [13]

Larry walks into that room, and anxiety and frustrations melt away. It's peace from the Holy Spirit that lives within

Larry and is clear to those around him. As Christians who seek to live the Great Commission in their workplaces, PTA boardrooms, and their community, it is critical we reflect the peace of God that is in us. Philippians 4:7 tells us, "And the peace of God, which transcends all understanding, will guard your hearts and your minds in Christ Jesus."

When Peace Feels Absent

It's hard to be a peacemaker in our homes or workplaces if we don't have peace inside us. I know I am out of sorts and short-tempered when I am not at peace. I'll admit, too often, I have raised my voice at my children because I left my office frustrated about someone else or something else at work. I'll admit that occasionally I have offered a trite comment in an office meeting that has inflamed a situation. When I reflect on these moments, I find that my frustration is most often because of my lack of peace. The lack of peace comes from a place of anxiety. While in my previous example with my hot-tempered leader, I did not know where the stress was coming from; through therapy and close friends, I realized that my anxiety was usually born out of fear. Fear of loss, fear of expected conflict, fear of an unreconciled situation, or fear of an overwhelming schedule, which I no doubt created myself.

I have improved at recognizing when I am struggling and not at peace. About four years ago, I spent a year in therapy. My therapist was amazing, and she helped me to pay attention to how I responded to anxieties and stressful situations. She helped me see where I was not at peace and where I was not abiding in faith. She taught me how to slow my reactions and listen to how my body responds to the situation. While I have nowhere near mastered that, I now have formative practices in place for when I notice I am not at peace or running on empty.

These five spiritually formative practices have been life-changing for me:

1. Several years ago, someone introduced me to Breath Prayers. Breath Prayers are brief prayers in sync with your breathing. I have learned to do breath prayers throughout the day. When I am experiencing anxiety, it is remarkably calming. The breath prayer I say the most often during anxiety goes like this:

   (While breathing in) God of transformative peace *(then breathing out)* give me the peace that surpasses all understanding.

   Mary Kate Morse says the following about breath prayers: "Breath prayers help us depend on the Spirit for help with our weaknesses. They are short prayers we repeat over and over when we need them. Usually, when we stumble, it is not during our set-aside prayer times, but during our busy working times. Therefore, breath prayers are a meaningful way to live by the Spirit."[14]

2. I have found the gift of contemplative prayer. I don't know how I journeyed so long in my faith without this practice. When I am stressed, I find guided prayer particularly helpful. The practice keeps me focused and ensures my mind

is not wandering. Podcasts are great for this. My friends and former coworkers developed my favorite contemplative prayer podcast, Reverend Faith Romasco and Jason Marsh. It is called *Exhale Prayer*. *Exhale Prayer* has been a go-to podcast for me for a while. Each episode is between ten and thirty minutes and allows me to decompress, take in the goodness of Scripture, and focus on the King rather than any anxiety. You can find *Exhale Prayer* on Spotify and Apple Podcasts.[15]

3. *Streams in the Desert* is a devotional that was first printed in 1925! Written by L.B. Cowman, it includes a passage from Scripture and morning and evening devotions. Publishers have reprinted it multiple times, and I even possess a copy from the 1950s that belonged to my great-grandmother. Whenever I am experiencing anxiety, I swap out whatever devotional I am reading and return to *Streams in the Desert*.[16]

4. Listen to worship music. The practice of worshiping God through song is calming, and for me, it is like breathing in God's peace as I worship and praise Him.

5. Get into nature. Going for a walk in the mountains or even outside in the neighborhood is calming. Moving my body while clearing my head through praise and worship or prayer refreshes my mind so that I can restart my day with a new outlook.

As you allow the Spirit to shine through your life, I pray you will fill your heart with peace and be known as a peace-maker to those around you.

Tips and Biblical Encouragement

People will take note when our hearts are at peace. Others will notice when we are walking in the Spirit and living a peaceful life. Let's look at the book of Proverbs as we reimagine what Spirit-led peace looks like in the workplace:

1. Peace in the workplace looks like someone who is slow to anger. When we walk in the Spirit, anger will not lurk under the surface, waiting to rear its head. Your coworkers would not describe you as easily angered but as someone with a calming presence.

    Do not make friends with a hot-tempered person, do not associate with one easily angered.

    — Proverbs 22:24

2. Be helpful to those around you. Have you ever worked with someone who was extraordinarily helpful? Does anyone come to mind? In the middle of the pandemic, we were doing a major conversion from Microsoft Office to G-Suite. One woman, Kim Berdyz, stood out as putting everyone before herself. Hundreds of people knew her simply for her desire to help others succeed.

Do not say to your neighbor, "Come back tomorrow and I'll give it to you"—when you already have it with you.

— Proverbs 3:28

3. Our words matter, and we must choose them wisely. Whether communicating hard information or reconciling a situation between multiple parties, be sure to speak thoughtfully. Recognizing the words you speak have impact and reflect the Kingdom of God.

The lips of the righteous nourish many, but fools die for lack of sense.

— Proverbs 10:21

4. Show humility, not arrogance. Our action and body language convey information about us. Do we interact with humility or do we show up with arrogance? Do we think we are the smartest person in the room, or do we engage with a spirit that seeks to understand others and their talents?

When pride comes, then comes disgrace, but with humility comes wisdom.

— Proverbs 11:2

5. Don't gossip. Gossip causes strife, and strife is the opposite of peace. I'm a great secret keeper, but I confess I can get sucked into gossip. As a secret keeper,

I'm not typically the teller of gossip, but I have been a listener too many times. Thanks be to God that He is not done with me yet. I have witnessed how gossip ruins lives in the workplace, and as Christians, we cannot take part in that.

A gossip betrays a confidence, but a trustworthy person keeps a secret.

— Proverbs 11:13

6. Encourage and lift your coworkers up. At my church, they used to call me the CEO, Chief Edification Officer. It was a joke because I could always be found encouraging the staff and congregants. When we uplift and motivate each other, we establish a sense of camaraderie, leading to a harmonious coexistence.

The soothing tongue is a tree of life, but a perverse tongue crushes the spirit.

— Proverbs 15:4

7. Listen to the feedback of others. Find mentors, and focus on growth and learning during your career. Take coaching from your leaders. If stuck, consider hiring a professional development coach. When you receive constructive criticism, don't take a defensive posture; listen and respond with grace.

Listen to advice and accept discipline, and at the end, you will be counted among the wise.

— Proverbs 19:20

8. Work hard and be reliable. In 2001, Rod Malone appointed me to my first formal leadership role. He was a leader who consistently showed hard work. I have worked with Rod for most of my professional career. He has been my boss, my customer, and a peer. When I think of reliability and hard work, I think of him. His firm commitment to getting things done is clear in his work ethic and willingness to always go the extra mile for the customer. No matter what, he responds and delivers.

Sluggards do not plow in season, so at harvest time they look but find nothing.

— Proverbs 20:4

9. Always do what is right. Integrity is at the center of our character as Christians. If you are in a situation and don't know what the right thing to do is, get a trusted partner to discern the next steps with you.

To do what is right and just is more acceptable to the Lord than sacrifice.

— Proverbs 21:3

10. Invest in the people you work with. My friend Laura Young-Shehata is the best person I know at this. As long as I have known Laura, she has been investing in the people she encounters. She doesn't do this only for work purposes; she wants to make a difference in their lives. Many have started in the corporate world because Laura recognized talent and took a chance on them.

As iron sharpens iron, so one person sharpens another.

— Proverbs 27:17

Reflective Questions

1. In what ways have you experienced or witnessed a lack of peace in your workplace? How did it impact your well-being and the team?

2. Reflecting on your experiences, how can you actively pursue peacemaking in your workplace? What steps can you take to move from being a passive observer to an active participant in creating peace?

3. How can you guard against gossip and ensure that your words build up rather than tear down?

4. Consider Romans 12:18, "If it is possible, as far as it depends on you, live at peace with everyone." How can you strive to maintain peace in difficult situations?

5. In what ways can your actions as a peacemaker at work reflect the Great Commission and be a witness to the love and peace of Christ?

CHAPTER 3
Patience

We choose to say no to certain pleasures, because patience is our guide in the Cruciform life.

—Derek Vreeland[17]

As I write on the fruit of the Spirit, I keep thinking that I will get to one I have mastered, but then along comes patience. In many ways, patience seems like an abandoned behavior. As a society, we aren't patient. When I want something, I want it now. It's why when ordering from Amazon, I select to see only Prime options. With Prime options, I can get whatever I want faster. Why should I wait longer than next-day delivery? When I can't get an item in a few days, I am frustrated, "Why is this taking so long?" I also have a subscription to Instacart, and I use both methods routinely. When I am hungry, pizza delivery isn't the only option anymore. I have a DoorDash account, which means I don't even have to drive to pick up my takeout; someone will pick it up and bring it to me. The other day I was ordering a gift for my friend, and when I realized I couldn't get it delivered the same day, I abandoned the order. Not only do I need instant gratification on my orders, but I also desire it when I send gifts!

When it comes to patience in the workplace, it can seem like it's evaporated right before our eyes. We want immediate responses to email, chat, and company socials. Our culture of immediate gratification creates emergencies when they are unnecessary, and it is often a source of stress. I get requests for information multiple times a day, and the people are often expecting an instant answer. Providing accurate and complete information would take me weeks of work, but people need the data now.

During a particularly stressful season, one of my leaders asked me for some information that I told him we didn't have. He was going to use it to make essential staffing decisions, and as I explained the complexity of getting this information, he got frustrated with our systems and ended up just telling me to guess. People's livelihoods were at stake, their families would be affected, and I was being asked to guess. I want to clarify that my leader wasn't responsible for it. He had pushed back to his leadership, but that fell on deaf ears. He trusted me and knew I would give him an educated guess with the best possible information. The reality was our systemic lack of patience and business drivers drove the immediacy of the request.

We are living in a world that is becoming increasingly impatient. I have been working on this book for about a year, and as I write each chapter, I follow a loose methodology.

1. I pray. I pray I will listen to the Spirit and that the Spirit will work through me as I write and that it will be impactful to others when they read it.

2. I begin free writing with whatever comes out onto the Google doc.
3. I read at least one excerpt from the Bible on the topic.
4. I research for helpful articles and sources.
5. I refer to books on specific topics.
6. I go back and rework the freewriting into a readable format.
7. I pause, pray, and revisit the writing (this is an iterative process).

Patience was the only fruit of the Spirit that came up with many tangible articles on how to train yourself in that specific characteristic. Of course, you can find articles on embodying the other behaviors, quick tips and ideas, but generally according to the many searches I performed, it seems that, unlike love, goodness, and joy, it is somewhat possible to train oneself to be patient. Interestingly enough, if you think about it, we all know a few techniques to help ourselves with patience.

How many times have we heard "count to ten before responding" or "take a few deep breaths"? We can use many tactics to improve our patience; chances are, you have tried a few of these yourself. Let's look at three sets of lists from some well-known organizations. Inc.com has four techniques to practice your patience:

1. Make yourself wait.
2. Stop doing things that aren't important.
3. Be mindful of the things making you impatient.
4. Relax and take deep breaths.[18]

The Cleveland Clinic gives us these six practices:

1. Practice mindfulness.
2. Know what's in your control.
3. Build your tolerance for discomfort.
4. Listen well.
5. Find the fun.
6. Empathize. [19]

NBC (DiGiulio) gives us three practices:

1. Identify when you are impatient and the emotion you are feeling.
2. Reframe how you think about the situation.
3. Think with your purpose in mind.[20]

These are all excellent methods for improving patience within ourselves. When we engage in intentional practices to strengthen our character, it is a sign of commitment to embody these characteristics of the Spirit in our lives. God desires our love and commitment, which means working to better ourselves and grow in Christ. Often, Christians minimize the value of practices outside of devotions, prayer, and church attendance. The truth is, we can learn from Inc.com, the Cleveland Clinic, NBC News, and others.

I may sit in my quiet time, read verses about patience, and ask my small church group to pray for me, but my efforts can't end there. Implementing moment-to-moment practices is necessary to improve ourselves in any of these biblical character traits. When we do this, we will grow in Christ-likeness.

Impatience Triggers

Certain things seem to make me impatient immediately. The reality is, just thinking about them irritates me and likely increases my blood pressure.

- People that always play devil's advocate. I understand we need to look at a problem or opportunity from various angles; however, we all know those people who will play the devil's advocate at all costs. It's exhausting, and it tries my patience.
- One-uppers. You likely know a few coworkers who are one-uppers. If someone has a good idea, they have a better one—every time.
- People who talk or ask questions just to hear themselves talk. I was recently in a meeting with one of these people, and I had several people message me asking if I could cut the person off because they were wasting everyone's time.
- Waiting on something that directly affects the people that work for me. Usually, this is because of an overly bureaucratic process.

I asked a group of people in different industries and roles what patience triggers they experienced at work. Here were some of the more common responses:

- Waiting or working through a lengthy process or procedure for something that should be simple.
- Unnecessary and disruptive changes that made things harder for them to complete their work.
- Waiting for an email or phone call response from a colleague.
- Having to forward information they have already sent because the receiver couldn't find it.
- Being asked to do busy work that is not meaningful.
- People not listening or responding because they are on their phone or listening to headphones.

I realize that in the examples mentioned above, more often than not, people are doing their best. I will often be heard saying, "Assume good intent." In these situations, if I remind myself that the person before me is operating from a place of good intent, my frustrations decrease and my patience increases. We encounter difficult people everywhere we go. It is part of our life, whether at work or home, and at times, each of us falls into this category. We can all become arduous, and if you think about it, most often it's our lack of patience that turns us into difficult people.

What Triggers Impatience in You?

I just listed many impatience triggers, but James S. Spiegel challenges us to describe patience without giving examples. He describes patience as "waiting without complaint."[21] I think complaining is the only thing that makes these moments bearable! I think he is right, though. Complaining certainly doesn't sound like patience, nor does it sound godly. If we want to become more like Christ, perhaps we should stop complaining. But how?

What if every time we caught ourselves complaining, we stopped and did silent prayers of thanksgiving and gratitude instead? I can see myself now, a little bit late, running into the airport and discovering that the TSA-PreCheck line is long. Instead of impatiently looking every two seconds to see what's taking so long, what if I adopted prayers of thanksgiving? It would look something like this:

> *God, thank You for a moment to pause in this chaotic day.*
> *God, thank You for a safe trip to the airport.*
> *God, thank You for keeping me safe as I prepare to fly.*
> *God, thank You for the breath in my lungs.*
> *God, thank You for the pilot of my aircraft.*

Simply the act of writing out this practice has been a source of patience and peacefulness for me. Gratitude is like that; when we enter the gates of thanksgiving, walls come down, patience levels rise, there is more joy in our hearts, and love overflows.

Pick one thing, make a mental note, and the next time you feel that urge to complain, instead pause and enter into a posture of thanksgiving. First Thessalonians 5:16–18 says, "Rejoice always, pray continually, give thanks in all circumstances; for this is God's will for you in Christ Jesus."

Biblical Patience

None of us desire to be impatient. I don't know anyone who wishes they had less patience than they do. Not only do I want to show patience with those I encounter, but I also genuinely want to feel patient. I want my anxiety to go down and for me to feel patience in my body. I want to live a life where the outflow of the Spirit is evident and contagious, and that includes the challenging fruit of patience. But biblical patience is so much deeper than the examples I just gave and likely the examples you noted. Biblical patience is about waiting on God. Biblical patience is about long-suffering.

Christopher Wright says that patience is "the ability to endure for a long time whatever opposition and suffering may come our way, and to show perseverance without wanting retaliation or revenge. The ability to put up with the weaknesses and foibles of others (including other believers), and to show forbearance toward them, without getting quickly irritated or angry enough to want to fight back."[22]

Let's look at some examples of patience in the Bible:

- Noah spent one hundred and twenty years building an ark.
- Sarah and Abraham waited twenty-five years after God promised them a child. Sarah was ninety, and Abraham was one hundred when Issaac was born.
- Samuel anointed David fifteen years before he became king.
- Hannah was barren for years but continued to believe that God would grant her a child. She

prayed and waited, and eventually, she became pregnant.

- Job is most well-known for remaining faithful during significant trials and suffering. While covered in sores and in constant pain, Job lost everything (including his home and family) but remained faithful to God throughout.

I don't know about you, but next to this list, I don't think the things that make me impatient stack up very well. In fact, the list above seems quite trivial as opposed to these examples from the Bible. These biblical stories are ones of long-suffering, and they expose our modern-day collective impatience. I would venture to say that our culture of impatience is an epidemic, and I think a lack of spiritual formation is the heart of the problem.

Spiritual Formation

Spiritual formation is the longest journey we will ever take, and if we are impatiently looking for shortcuts, we will miss out on all that God has intended for us. While each chapter in this book includes formative spiritual practices, the act of spiritual formation itself requires patience. In this chapter, we will unpack spiritual formative practices; after all, forming ourselves into Christlikeness is a lifelong process. In Discovering Discipleship, Dean Blevins and Mark Maddox remind us, "The idea of faith formation as a continuous process that requires patience and endurance contrasts with our society's focus on instant gratification. The Christian journey, therefore, describes an intentional and continual commitment to a lifelong process of growth toward wholeness in Christ."[23]

As workers in God's glorious story of redemption, we must take part daily in spiritually formative practices. To be actively formed, we need to be intentional in formation in the ordinary sacred moments in our life.

Tish Warren Harrison wrote a book a few years ago called *The Liturgy of the Ordinary*. She wrote about sacred practices in ordinary tasks like making your bed, losing your keys, sitting in traffic, and reading emails. While most people I know immediately started making their beds (I did, too), the chapter that captivated me was on checking one's email. Harrison notes she is always behind in email, making her feel like a failure, but checking her email is holy. Some may say this is over-spiritualizing; I think I thought that the first time I read it, but she reminds us that each week when we leave our houses of worship, we are sent out into the world for ordinary and holy tasks. Harrison says, "This kingdom vision-our identity as those blessed and sent-must work itself out in the small routines of our daily work and vocation, as we go to meetings, check our email, make our children dinner, or mow the lawn. While our methods of interaction, like email, may be modern, it is still holy work."[24]

Brothers and sisters, if you think your job has nothing to do with ministry, you are wrong. You are on a mission for God's Kingdom every moment of the day.

If email can be a sacred, ordinary task, it seems to me that if we are being intentional about our spiritual formation, just about anything we do could be holy.

As we relate formation to patience, it's important for us to recognize that patience means we have to set other tasks aside in order to be formed. One practice I have found to guide my formation is through what I call the worship reset.

In the middle of my day, when I feel patience (or peace) waning, I do a worship reset. The intent of this reset is to get me back to feeling God's presence. I have three songs that I rotate for my worship reset. I stop whatever I am doing and pick one of the three songs. I have been using this practice for a long time, and for years it was only one song, a 1980s Christian song by Dave Browning called "Take Me In." More recently, I added Elevation Worship's "Here Again and Yours."

These aren't my favorite worship songs, but I chose them because they always make me feel instantly like I am in the presence of God.

The worship reset allows me to take a 4-to-7-minute pause where I can practice patience and detach myself from whatever challenge or frustration I am experiencing. It's a reminder that spreadsheets, divisive meetings, or workplace drama don't hold power over me. There is only one King, and it's not the CEO, CFO, director, or customer. A worship pause enables me to return to work with a renewed spirit and mind. What might this look like in the workplace?

For a moment, simply imagine what more patience in your company, at your home office, in your cubicle, and in your meetings would look like.

Perhaps it would be like:

- More deep breaths, fewer responses out of anger.

- More focus on what people are saying and less on formulating our response.
- Realistic expectations, instead of causing undue stress by rushed timelines.
- More acknowledgment of effort, even if not all the results are clear.
- Allowing colleagues to finish speaking, not jumping in before they are finished.
- Apologies when we catch ourselves being impatient.

What other ways could you exhibit holiness where you work and with the people you work with? Right now, this practice of allowing your mind to imagine is spiritually formative.

The spiritual practices that I most consistently follow are:

1. Prayer Walks: While I typically work remotely, I do prayer walks whenever I am in an office or a physical work location. While I am walking, I pray for each of the areas listed here:

   - Company leaders
   - Company performance
   - Wisdom for me as I lead
   - Ways for me to evangelize
   - Prayers for the specific place I am at, people, mission, and because I work in hospitals, our patients

2. I slow down: Instead of making a five-minute rushed phone call or responding to emails, I often intentionally slow down between meetings by reading, taking a five-minute walk, or listening to worship music.

3. I set aside intentional time for the sacred ordinary task of email. I make email an event in my day rather than something I spend every free minute doing.

4. I rest. I no longer work every moment; instead, I remind myself that one of the Ten Commandments is to remember the Sabbath day and keep it holy. Sabbath is the act of embodying rest for the mind, body, and soul, and it is an intentional act of faithfulness in our lives. I look forward to regular Sabbath, and it doesn't always look the same for me. It may be a scheduled massage, a hike in the mountains, or an extended connection time with a friend.

The Movement of God Requires Our Patience

I have noticed that we get impatient when we don't see progress as we would like, whether specifically for the mission of God, a particular project at work, or our home life. Six months go by without an invitation to do something bigger or better, and you equate that to no progress in your career. Maybe what you are working on right now is paving the way for something more significant in the future. Perhaps God has plans for you to stay exactly where you are for the next fifteen years. We don't know, but we must not let our impatience drive us in a direction that is not God's desire for us.

When I think of patience, I think about the patience God must have with us. Are we just part of a bunch of fledgling churches or a great commission that has been reduced to a good commission? Take a look at church history. Look into how your church started and you will see the hand of God woven throughout. The Church in Spain is a good example for us; it traces its origins back to the Apostle James. James is often credited with bringing Christianity to the region in the first century. That's a long time ago, and over the centuries, the Church has grown despite going through regime changes and intensely complex periods. Through each era, the Church has had to adapt and persevere, patiently rebuilding and nurturing its influence despite many challenges. This patience has been key to its enduring legacy, visible today in Spain's grand cathedrals and lasting traditions, symbolizing a faith that has shaped Spanish culture over centuries. The movement of God, whether it be in a small office or on a global scale, requires our patience and perseverance, remembering that it won't be complete until Christ comes again.

Tips and Biblical Encouragement

1.   Leave the behaviors of complaining and dissatisfaction to others.

   Do everything without grumbling or arguing, so that you may become blameless and pure, "children of God

without fault in a warped and crooked generation."
Then you will shine among them like stars in the sky.

— Philippians 2:14–15

2. Be patient while waiting for God's timing, not ours.
    We may desire that next promotion, job change, or
    commendation, but it may not be in God's timing. Be
    hopeful, prepare yourself, but focus on the job before
    you while being prayerfully patient for the future.

    But if we hope for what we do not yet have, we wait
    for it patiently.

— Romans 8:25

3. Spiritual formation is lifelong. Take your growth in
    Christ seriously and integrate it into your work life.

    I thank my God every time I remember you. In all my
    prayers for all of you, I always pray with joy because of
    your partnership in the gospel from the first day until
    now, being confident of this, that he who began a good
    work in you will carry it on to completion until the
    day of Christ Jesus.

— Philippians 1:3–6

4. Practice patience in your work and you will produce
    more wisdom and fewer mistakes.

Patience leads to abundant understanding, but impatience leads to stupid mistakes.

— Proverbs 14:29

5. Show patience and discernment with evangelism. Sometimes we can desire others to become Christians so badly we become annoying evangelizers and turn people away from God. We can't coerce people into following Jesus. Rather, it's living our lives in a way that is attractive to others, and it's being wise in how we share the love of Jesus.

The Lord is not slow in keeping his promise, as some understand slowness. Instead, he is patient with you, not wanting anyone to perish but everyone to come to repentance.

— 2 Peter 3:9

6. Consciously recognize and be patient with difficult people you encounter. Nothing says a lack of patience like someone who is quick to anger.

Whoever is patient has great understanding, but one who is quick-tempered displays folly.

— Proverbs 14:29

7. Don't jump to conclusions, but consider the perspectives of others. Often, we can become impatient with others because we are looking at a situation myopically. When

we are seeking to understand the viewpoint of the other, it can change our perspective.

For my thoughts are not your thoughts, neither are your ways my ways, declares the LORD.

— Isaiah 55:8

Reflective Questions

1. How does practicing patience in daily life reflect the character of Jesus and His teachings?
2. In what ways can you demonstrate patience as an act of love and service to others, fulfilling the Great Commission?
3. What practical steps can you take to cultivate patience in situations where you typically feel frustrated or hurried?
4. How can adopting a posture of thanksgiving, instead of complaining, transform your response to delays or challenges?
5. In what ways can your workplace become a mission field where patience is a testimony to your faith?
6. How does understanding patience as "waiting without complaint" challenge your current attitude toward setbacks and disappointments?
7. How does viewing ordinary tasks as sacred opportunities for spiritual formation change your approach to everyday life?

CHAPTER 4

Kindness

Kindness. Language which the dumb can speak, and the deaf can understand.

— Christian Nestell Bovee[25]

I am writing this morning from a campground in San Clemente, California. My amazing parents took my kids to the San Diego Wild Animal Park. So right now, I am teenager-less, my husband is asleep in our RV, and I am sitting at a picnic table with a stack of books, my iPad, and a fantastic cup of drip coffee from Zebra House Coffee. It's February 19, 2022, and it's 64 degrees. I can feel a very light breeze on my face, and as my friend Tara says, "I can hear the trees singing praises to the Lord" as they sway back and forth with the wind. The sun shines through a large eucalyptus tree, giving me the perfect amount of warmth. Birds are chirping and singing from the trees that surround me. I think there must be dozens of bird species here from the unique sounds. In the tree to my left is a hummingbird sporting a bright red belly; its distinctive hum is loud as it investigates the dainty orange flowers on the tree. Many plant and tree varieties are present. I can see purple, yellow, orange, and blue flowers from my seat. A vibrant shade of blue paints the sky. The landscape is lush with many shades of green. In the distance, I can see the sun shimmering off the Pacific Ocean. God has blessed me with the sounds, weather, view, breeze on my face, and the perfect cup of coffee.

I have always been in awe of God's majestic work in creation. How many times have you heard the phrase "this is God's country" when someone describes an exceptionally beautiful landscape? As long as I can remember, I have been in awe of the earth's beauty, but I have never thought of nature as a sign of God's loving kindness until now. In its simplicity and grandeur, nature is a loving and kind gift to us from God.

I have three brothers. My brother Matt has a sign up in his house that says, "Be nice or leave." I'm not big on rules, but I can easily get behind that one. Kindness is about attitude; kindness is about our approach and how we treat ourselves and those around us. If I were to describe my brother, I'd say he is kind, fair, no drama, and fun. My kids always enjoy going to Uncle Matt's house. In his work as one of the nation's top soccer trainers, athletes and parents alike adore him. It's more than just his soccer talent. Matt is kind and actively avoids getting caught up in the drama that is often present in competitive youth sports programs. He's earned a reputation for his kindness both on and off the field.

My two youngest siblings, Andrew and James, have spent a good portion of their working lives in the hospitality industry. Early in their careers, they worked for a variety of popular restaurants in the San Gabriel Valley of Southern California. Hospitality industry stories, restaurants in particular, showcase stories from extreme kindness to extreme vitriol. I have heard plenty of these anecdotes from these two former servers. Years ago, I heard a story about an executive who conducted all of their interviews at restaurants. A determining factor in his hires was how the candidate interacted with and treated the server assigned to their table.

In an article in the *Guardian*, Rachel Cooke notes, "I remember my grandmother telling me that if I were ever to marry, I should make sure he was kind. But she might just as well have said: 'Find yourself a man who's nice to waiters.' The way people treat restaurant staff is, I think, a kind of poker tell, revealing a person's character in as long as it takes to say: "I'll have the sea bass." A man (or woman) who is actively unpleasant to waiters is best avoided. Ditto those who patronize them. Just as bad, though, are people who treat waiters as though they're invisible. This is not, as these cretins seem to think, a sign of metropolitan sophistication."[26]

Last year, my friend and I were in Nashville at the same time and met for dinner. We hadn't seen each other in months, and we were talking to our waitress about how we were catching up over dinner. During our conversation, she told us she hadn't seen her best friend in over eight years. On the spot, we decided we were going to leave her a big enough tip for her to fly to visit her best friend. The waitress was both shocked and delighted! The act was about her feelings, not just the big tip. She regretted not seeing her friend. We saw the pain in her eyes, and at that moment, on both of our paydays, we made her day with a random act of kindness. More often than not, kindness is about how we make people feel seen. Just as we see with nature, kindness can be big or small.

My friend Anna Turman has been a hospital CEO and an IT CIO, but more than her titles, Anna is a lifter of others. I have never met someone who spends as much time as Anna writing notes of gratitude and encouragement to others. I have received mail from her more times than I can count. While a simple note would be lovely, Anna uses her creative gifts to send personalized, one-of-a-kind cards. She uses photos she has taken and hand-drawn images on the front of the card before writing her sentiments. Every time I see an envelope from Anna arrive in the mail, it brings me joy. Her practices are intentional, and they make people feel good. I often wonder how many individuals receive encouragement from Anna in a given week. How many employees kept going because Anna told them they matter?

One day I approached Anna and told her what a difference her cards made to me and many others. With some encouragement, she decided to start a business so that her creations could edify people more broadly. Anna now has a side hustle on Etsy called LeadInk, which encourages the "Art of Leadership & Engagement" through inspirational cards. We live in a world marred with discouragement. When we intentionally encourage and edify others, we remind them of their inherent worth.

Lack of Kindness Also Bears Witness

We aren't perfect. As broken, sinful people, we won't always show kindness in every situation. I remember one particular incident vividly. To set the stage, throughout the past twenty-five years, I've been constantly on the move for work. I typically fly over thirty-five round trips a year, and I am unwaveringly loyal to the businesses that assist me during my time away from home. Southwest Airlines, Hilton, Lyft, National

Car Rental—I couldn't live without you. I have the highest Southwest status, A-List Preferred, and have held their coveted companion pass since 2005.

In March 2014, I flew to Denver with my two young daughters and niece to meet my new nephew. It was my niece Elizabeth's first flight. She was six, and we were so excited to take her on the trip. My daughters were used to flying. They had their matching travel backpacks on and their boarding passes out. The three of them were lined up behind me in the A boarding group line.

As I approached the gate agent, she stated we needed to wait until family boarding. I told her we shouldn't need to, that per Southwest policy, the girls were supposed to board with the person carrying the A boarding pass. She disagreed, and my voice began to rise. I cited my Southwest status and previous experiences boarding with my kids. I asked her to call a supervisor, and as we continued to argue, she continued boarding other passengers. I was furious and lost my temper. I was obnoxious. When the A boarding group finished, she inquired if I wanted to board with my family or wait for the supervisor. I snarkily told her we would board. She scanned our boarding passes, and we walked to the plane. I was angry, and I knew she was wrong. We boarded the plane.

Once I had the girls situated in their seats, I sat down in mine. I was so mad; I was almost shaking. I pulled up the Southwest website and read the policy. It validated I was right, but as I sat there, I began to tear up. A flight attendant approached me and asked if I was okay. I said, "No, I just yelled at your gate agent." She said, "Well, hopefully, you feel better," and I replied, "No, I feel terrible. I treated her poorly, and it was unfair." Being right didn't matter anymore. The only thing that mattered was that I used my status to berate the gate agent. My friend Laura always reminds me that there is a cost to being right. There was a cost of being right here. I ruined someone's day and failed to reflect the Kingdom's way.

Some weeks later, while at the airport, I noticed the gate agent nearby. She was alone. I paused and then approached her to apologize. She saw me, and I said, "I'm sure you must remember me. I yelled at you a couple of weeks ago when I was boarding a flight to Denver."

She greeted me and said, "Yes, I do, and I want to talk to you."

I responded, "I just want to apologize. You didn't deserve the way I treated you, and I am really sorry."

The gate agent, Oana, responded, "But you were right! We checked with our supervisors and realized that our internal policy wasn't matching with what we had posted externally on the website. You were right!"

I told her, "It didn't matter if I was right. It didn't justify the way I talked to you. It was wrong. You were trying to do your job, and I didn't make it easy on you; I probably ruined your day, and I hope you can forgive me."

This story has a happy ending. Oana and I turned those horrible first impressions into a genuine friendship. I adore her. She has watched my children grow up, toured my kids on the Southwest planes, and even brought them gifts from her trip home to Romania. On my part, I consistently check in on what is happening in her life. Every time I am at the airport, I check every gate, hoping to find her, and we are even friends on social media. We are always excited to see each other, and we often laugh at how our friendship started. Despite our confrontational first interaction, I am fairly certain that Oana would call me a kind and Christlike person. As Christians, we will mess up. We will have moments where we don't look like the God we are supposed to represent. When that happens, it's up to us to listen to the promptings of the Spirit, exercise humility, repent, and work toward reconciliation.

In This World, Kindness Stands Out

Have you ever met someone and immediately knew they were extraordinarily gifted? In 2006, I met someone that wowed me, Laura Young-Shehata. At the time, I was employed by Perot Systems, and Laura was a newly appointed leader in the company. She had an energy that was unmatched by anyone I knew. She possessed fire and charisma, and people naturally gravitated towards her. As I got to know Laura, I realized that there was something very special about her, and we became fast friends. She is the most thoughtful person I know. Laura's countless acts of kindness could fill an entire book. It's constant; whether it is celebrating the successes of others, gifting plane tickets, or finding a job for someone who needs one, Laura shows up for people. She remembers birthdays, anniversaries, children's names, and where people are from. Laura cares about the details in people's lives and cultivates meaningful relationships with them. She shows kindness individually and broadly, not seeking accolades, but because she naturally reflects the image of God and uses her gifts and resources to benefit others.

It's people like Laura that you encounter in the market-place that are different. People like Laura spread contagious kindness that is seen across all levels of the organization. Who do you know that stands out? Take a moment and tell them today.

One day, I looked at my calendar, and I had a one-on-one meeting scheduled with a name I didn't recognize. The meeting invitation did not have a subject nor did it include content. I asked my executive assistant what the meeting topic was, and she didn't know, so I joined cold. I logged into the Zoom call and didn't recognize the person on the other end. She didn't work for me and I introduced myself. She said, "Thank you for taking this meeting. I need to talk to a senior leader who was kind, and I heard that it was you." She wanted to talk to me because I was kind. I immediately thought that was a low bar.

The ministry I was working for, CommonSpirit Health, trademarked the phrase "hello humankindness." The employees pride themselves on showing kindness to coworkers, patients, and the world. Learning that an IT professional wanted to speak with me because of my reputation for kindness felt like a punch in the gut. We were better than that! I spent the next thirty minutes talking with the team member about her struggles at work, her career aspirations, how I thought her work mattered, and how her skills could benefit the ministry in the future. She was genuinely grateful that I invested time in getting to know her, and I could see how she was encouraged by the recognition that she contributed to our mission. One thing we can do to show others kindness is to give them our time.

Her experience didn't reflect the organization's mission. In our department, the lack of clear kindness in that particular season was due to many factors. Companies experience ups and downs, but our assignment is to shine even in the darkest times. Our responsibility is to embody God's kindness in our daily interactions, regardless of the external circumstances.

In 2016, Lloyd Dean, the CEO of Dignity Health, told this story:

> *One of the most poignant moments of connection I can share is a story about a housekeeper at one of our hospitals who entered a patient's room to clean it. The patient was recovering from breast cancer surgery, and she was in pain. As she lay there in bed, she began to share her experience with the housekeeper and was surprised to learn that the housekeeper had also recovered from breast cancer surgery. The two connected and shared their stories. Months later, the patient would write to say that the clinical care she received was excellent, but it was the housekeeper that truly saved her life. She said the housekeeper gave her hope. Just like that housekeeper, we all have the opportunity to turn a chance meeting into a transformative experience. We can stop waiting for a national dialogue to take root and instead sow its seeds through small acts of kindness that lead to lasting change. We can stop doubting the intentions of strangers, and we can start bravely leading with kindness. Extending a hand and a smile, first, fostering a culture of compassion."[27]*

In 2006, Blake Myciskie introduced the "One for One" business model: for every pair of TOMS shoes sold, TOMS would donate a pair to a child in need. Blake Mycoskie's approach to kindness is evident in his business philosophy. He believes in integrating giving into the core of business operations, demonstrating that companies can be profitable while making a positive social impact. This perspective has influenced other businesses to adopt similar models, blending commerce with compassion.[28]

Advocating for people and justice is part of kindness. Whether it is a Catholic healthcare system, a retail store, or a small business, supporting organizations that advocate for health and justice for all makes incremental differences to those who are burdened. These companies know that the most powerful catalyst for change is found within each of us—and as such; they empower their teams to deliver their services in human-centric ways, and they shower people with kindness.

Being *for* People

"I've got your back." Chances are you have said this to someone or have had someone say it to you before. We've all heard it; it's a common phrase around workplaces, families, and friends. Knowing someone has your back and supports you is comforting, but wholeheartedly rooting for them is different. Having one's back implies that if someone is in trouble, you will defend them. You will stand beside them, but what would happen if we kicked that up a notch? Imagine for a moment that instead of having one's back, you told them you were *for* them. I am *for* you takes having one's back much further. It means that I am looking out for you. I am your advocate. I am working on your behalf.

In March 2022, I had the pleasure of visiting Neighborhood Church in Visalia, California. I have been in many churches across the United States, but I knew it was different the second I walked into it. Their signage made it crystal clear they exist to be "*For* Visalia." I had been telling my team that I was "*For* them" long before I visited this church, but I was awestruck when I saw the passion behind their mission. The people at Neighborhood Church are *for* each other, *for* their community, and *for* the Kingdom of God. I turned to my friend and said, "I would move to Visalia *for* this church. This is a community I would love to be a part of." Their lead pastor, Forrest Jenan, told us about how they practice and embody being *For* Visalia. It is through tangible acts to improve their community, caring for foster children, and cultivating a culture of hospitality with their neighbors. Imagine our workplaces and imagine our witness if those we encountered knew we were *for* them!

Last year, one of my beloved team members came to me with another job opportunity. Michael had worked his way from a contracted end-user support technician to his current role as the Director of our system offices. He felt the gravity of his role, and the knowledge that his departure would create a significant void for our team weighed heavily on him. He went through the ways this would cause a burden for his team and me, and as he did, he started to cry. We got along great; leaving me and the group that formed him would not be easy. I began to tear up; Michael was like family to me in many ways. With tears in my eyes, I looked at him and said, "You know, I am in the Michael Frazier business. I am *for* you. This sounds like an amazing opportunity." We talked, I helped him discern the new role, and together we came up with a list of pros and cons. When it looked like it would be a good move for him and his family, I told him to go after it.

When we hung up the FaceTime call, I dialed the hiring manager. I told him what a rock star Michael was and encouraged the leader to hire him. I was *for* Michael. He now serves as the director of a cybersecurity team. Two years into the job change, Michael and I continue to connect. He knows that being *for* him didn't stop when he moved to his new job; there is a history of trust between us, and we make an effort to maintain our relationship. The highest level of trust in the workplace is when your colleagues know you are with them in the trenches of their jobs and you are *for* them in their lives.

Workplace Kindness

In 2021 *Harvard Business Review* noted that we shouldn't underestimate the power of kindness at work. The article highlights that decades of research have proven that recognition at work goes a long way toward improving employee well-being. Specifically, the article states, "Receiving a compliment, words of recognition, and praise can help individuals feel more fulfilled, boost their self-esteem, improve their self-evaluations, and trigger positive emotions. These positive downstream consequences of compliments make intuitive sense: Praise aligns with our naturally positive view of ourselves, confirming our self-worth."[29] Knowing the effects of recognition, we as Christians should not withhold feedback, and instead, we should be generous with our commendations. We should be wise in how we recognize our colleagues to avoid appearing disingenuous. Rather than anything else, our aim is to provide valuable feedback and recognition, which lifts people up and satisfies our innate need for appreciation. I challenge each of us to strive to give timely, thorough, and thoughtful feedback.

In the same way, we recognize each other; we need to remember that if we are in a position to help others, at times, we need to give constructive criticism. Not only is it necessary, but it is also the kind thing to do. Some of us have a tendency to avoid providing negative feedback because it doesn't feel comfortable. I can raise my hand at this. I have a tendency to put off giving undesirable feedback because I don't want to hurt the person's feelings or bring them down. Despite my good intentions, there is no kindness in this. We must help others be the best version of themselves, and if we don't provide constructive feedback, we can't help them grow and refine. I believe that if I had honed this skill earlier in my career, it would have benefited the people who worked on my teams more.

To kindly provide real feedback in the workplace, you need to know the people you work with. Recently, I heard a story about an exceptional performer who received a less-than-stellar review. This person is highly competent, kind, and responsible. He is one of the best I've worked with in my career. He is great at his job, and his reviews have always reflected his commitment, excellence, and overall stellar performance. No doubt he has become accustomed to accolades. Last year, he went through a transition that removed several layers of leadership and the local leader at his location. He stepped up, filled all the gaps that were left, and did so with his usual commitment to his team and customers. When it came time for his performance review, he expected to hear his new leader's appreciation; instead, his review was mediocre. He told him he didn't know him well enough to rate him differently than average. The reviewer neglected to inquire, review past feedback, or familiarize himself with his achievements before the meeting. Whether giving or receiving feedback, we all need to do our homework. It's the fair and kind thing to do.

Knowing your audience isn't something you can learn when it's time to give feedback. Curiosity drives the ongoing process of forming relationships with colleagues. Get to know people and establish trust with them. When you give them feedback, it's more likely they will take it in the manner intended, even if it's negative. You want the receiver to know, whether positive or negative, that you are telling them because you have their best interest in mind. Depending on the person, when I need to give undesirable feedback, I begin by affirming their gifts and then getting specific on the feedback for the situation. This ongoing feedback is helpful to ensure they are growing. People will work towards becoming the best version of themselves if they receive prompt, honest feedback. Helping people grow is kind. I would be remiss if I left out what Brene Brown often says, "Clear is kind, unclear is unkind."[30]

One of my executive partners, Lisa McClaine, has over thirty-five years of experience with large corporations and technology companies from MCI to Unisys. Besides her corporate experiences, she spent ten years leading her own consulting firm. Lisa's brilliance, ingenuity, and kindness drew me to her. I asked Lisa about her secret to kindness in the marketplace, and she said, "Kindness means many things to many people.

To me, it means empathy. It means taking time to listen and really understand where others are coming from. It means listening to every side of a story and leading by example." She wrote this example:

> Years ago, my boss came to me and told me he wanted to transfer a difficult employee into my department. My boss said this person hadn't worked out in other groups and it was up to me to decide if we kept this person or let them go. He thought this person had potential…but so many people complained that my boss was actually told by his leader to let this person go. When this person joined my group, I met with him. I wanted to learn his "side of the story." I asked him about his frustrations, his goals, his strengths, his weaknesses. As a leader, we quickly learn. We all have weaknesses. I always try to put teams together where the team is stronger than the individual. What I learned was this person was close to genius technically (not kidding) – but was not good at documenting or good at writing out a plan. Instead of expecting this employee to do something he would never succeed at, I listened, I learned, and I surrounded him with others who would help him succeed. We became good friends. He worked for me for over 20 years across multiple companies because I treated him with kindness instead of pre-judging based on what others thought. Living a Christian life is not about the situations we encounter; it's about how we choose to react to those situations.

Choosing kindness means living a life of empathy
without regret. It means following in Jesus's footsteps.[31]

By taking the kindness path, Lisa shows what it looks like demonstrating Jesus's kindness to others. The Spirit of the Living God, who works in each of us, enables our light to shine brighter than it would otherwise.

Tips and Biblical Encouragement

How else can we show kindness in the workplace? If we are representing our Heavenly Father, I can only imagine that we want to show basic courtesy and love, but kindness goes much further than politeness. Sure, we want to say things like please and thank you. Sure, we want to make requests versus demands. Of course, kindness includes being respectful to others. But beyond being courteous, well-mannered, and showing basic human decency, there are more habits of kindness that we as Christians need to form:

1.   Put others before yourself. Reverend Tara Beth Leach often says, "You first."

Do nothing out of selfish ambition or vain conceit.
Rather, in humility, value others above yourselves.

— Philippians 2:3

2.   Be respectful.

Respect everyone, and love the family of believers.
Fear God and respect the king.

— 1 Peter 2:17

3.   Do not refrain from speaking ill of one another but actually lift others up. I have a relatively recent practice of sending a Friday email to someone that is intentionally meant to build them up.

Do not let any unwholesome talk come out of your mouths, but only what is helpful for building others up according to their needs, that it may benefit those who listen.

— Ephesians 4:29

4.   The Golden Rule: treat others as you would like to be treated. Another way of saying this is don't treat people poorly.

And as you wish that others would do to you, do so to them.

— Luke 6:31

5.   Provide for the needs of others.

The islanders showed us unusual kindness. They built a fire and welcomed us all because it was raining and cold.

— Acts 28:2

6.   Show up for others.

And is well known for her good deeds, such as bringing up children, showing hospitality, washing the feet of the Lord's people, helping those in trouble and devoting herself to all kinds of good deeds.

— 1 Timothy 5:10

Reflective Questions

1.   In what ways does our attitude towards others reflect the kindness of God?
2.   How can we cultivate a spirit of encouragement and support, as Anna does with her cards, to lift others up in our communities?
3.   When we fail to show kindness, how can we seek forgiveness and reconciliation to align with the teachings of Christ?
4.   How can we intentionally be "for" others, advocating for their success and well-being, as an expression of loving our neighbor?
5.   Consider Philippians 2:3: "Do nothing out of selfish ambition or vain conceit. Rather, in humility, value others above yourselves." How does our treatment of strangers reveal our character and witness as Christians?

CHAPTER 5

Goodness

Human greatness does not lie in wealth or power, but in character and goodness. People are just people, and all people have faults and shortcomings, but all of us are born with a basic goodness.

— Anne Frank[32]

Dictionary.com defines goodness:

- the state or quality of being good.
- moral excellence; virtue.
- kindly feeling; kindness; generosity.
- excellence of quality:
- goodness of workmanship.
- the best part of anything; essence; strength.[33]

God is good, and the goodness that is in us comes from God. When we walk in the Spirit, we will exhibit the characteristics of God. What does that look like in human form today? It looks like someone who is honest, someone who has integrity, someone who does the right thing. Christopher J.H. Wright explored the heart of goodness, and he describes it this way: "I think one key thing would be integrity—an absence of any kind of guile or deception. Truly good people are WYSIWYG (What You See Is "What You Get)."[34] In other words, good people are authentic.

In the fall of 2022, a major cybersecurity attack hit the organization I worked for. It was the first of its kind to impact our organization, and everyone had to pitch in. I was the information technology leader responsible for teams at all our locations. Because of this, they included me in a very small group of executive leaders who were tracking the problem at the system level. I will never forget when the CFO, Daniel Morrisette, asked to speak. I expected him to ask questions about patient billing; I expected him to inquire about accounts receivable; I expected him to talk about how this was going to hurt our cash on hand. I expected him to ask us to estimate how much this was going to cost, but he didn't say any of those things. Dan said, "I don't want any of you to worry about the financial implications of this right now. We must put our patients first, and we need to focus all of our energy on taking care of the people." I sat there with nothing but admiration. This was goodness.

As Christopher Wright described WYSIWYG, he said, "When they do good, it is not just some kind of playacting to get a good name, or a good photo op, or a good sound bite. Good people do what they do simply because it is the right thing to do. Goodness is close to what it means to be pure in heart."[35]

Doing the Right Thing

The right thing is not always obvious. I hate to admit that I have to discern the right thing more often than I would like. While I am committed to doing what is right, sometimes I wrestle with what the right thing to do actually is. Early in my career, my boss called me and coerced me into lying about a human resources incident. He would have been in serious trouble had I not backed up his side of the story. When I was called by human resources, I supported him and lied. I knew I shouldn't, but I was young and scared. I have regretted that decision ever since.

Many years later, a superior asked me to make a statement that was not truthful to another leader. Of course, the superior didn't put it that way, but as I looked at the situation, I knew I was being asked to fabricate. From the very beginning, I knew I wouldn't lie. I would never make that mistake again, but I wrestled with whether the right thing to do was to report the superior to human resources or not. I had compassion for the person; they were in trouble, and they were trying to save their neck. Nevertheless, I was being asked to do something that, if I were to comply, would compromise my integrity.

I consulted my husband and trusted advisors about the situation so that they could help me discern the right path forward. After listening to their feedback, praying, and reflecting, I ultimately concluded that the request made of me was not only morally inappropriate but also an abuse of power. I knew the right thing to do was to contact our HR department and report the situation. It was uncomfortable; I didn't want to do it, but I knew that if I was going to look at myself in the mirror, if I was going to practice goodness, if I was going to model integrity, I needed to report it. The leader I spoke to in HR assured me I did the right thing. He affirmed my action was appropriate, and I left the meeting with peace, knowing that no matter what happened next, I did the right thing.

A Biblical Role Model

As I was researching goodness, I repeatedly came back to the story of Daniel in the Bible. Daniel's story is incredible. While most know the story of Daniel and the lion's den, there is so much more to Daniel than this dramatic and amazing story of God's protection.

In *Cultivating the Fruit of the Spirit*, Christopher JH Wright said: "If God is utterly good, then it's not surprising that people who live close to God reflect his character and are marked by this same quality. Daniel is a good example of goodness in action. Daniel held positions of power and authority in Babylon."[36]

Daniel was a political administrator. He worked for multiple government agencies, and the Bible says in Daniel 6:3–4 that his enemies could find no corruption in him. Wright elaborated on Daniel's qualities, emphasizing a spirit of excellence in his work and the trust he garnered from his leader and subordinates. He said, "His goodness and integrity were transparent and evident to all."[37]

That, my friends, is what we should strive for. When goodness and integrity are within us, our colleagues, our customers, and others who surround us will see that goodness, and we will reflect the good kingdom of God. We all know

Daniels, people we see in action who consistently show goodness and integrity and who we know are trustworthy.

Original Goodness

Despite being sinners from the start, we are still capable of goodness. I was raised with the belief that I could attribute my goodness solely to asking Jesus into my heart and receiving His gift of salvation. As I grew up, this teaching confused me. I met non-Christians, atheists, and Muslims who were good people. I met agnostics who fed the poor every week and Christians who ignored the poor. This concept wasn't reconciling with me, so I dug into Scripture rather than culture.

Genesis 1:27 says, "So God created mankind in his own image, in the image of God he created them; male and female He created them." J.L. Packer said, "This passage shows us, first, our unique and special dignity (God speaks of no creature other than man as his image-bearer), and, second, how we are meant to live."[38]

The fall of creation occurs in Genesis 3. Genesis 3 tells the story of Adam and Eve's disobedience in the Garden of Eden. The serpent tricked Eve into eating the forbidden fruit, leading to Adam also partaking. Their act of defiance results in their awareness of good and evil. God confronts them, they pass blame, and then they receive consequences: the serpent is cursed, Adam and Eve receive a list of curses, and they are thrown out of the garden of Eden. When God delivers the list of curses, He says nothing about them no longer being created in His image.

The concept of being made in God's image implies we are meant to embody qualities similar to God's. This means acting with wisdom and being purposeful in our actions. Just as God generated goodness in creation, we are called to create value in our work. Packer takes it a step further, telling us just as God blessed Adam and Eve, we are to show love and goodwill to all people.

Richard Rohr explores what it means to have original goodness. He wrote:

> Our inherent "likeness to God" depends upon the objective connection given by God equally to all creatures, each of whom carries the divine DNA in a unique way. Owen Barfield called this phenomenon "original participation." I would also call it "original blessing" or "original innocence" ("unwoundedness").*
>
> Whatever you call it, the "image of God" is absolute and unchanging. There is nothing humans can do to increase or decrease it. And it is not ours to decide who has it or does not have it, which has been most of our problem up to now. It is a pure and total gift, given equally to all.[39]

Rohr explains that the concept of Original Sin was first introduced by Augustine in the fifth century and, with it, the complexity it brought to original goodness. Rohr continues:

> After Augustine, most Christian theologies shifted from the positive vision of Genesis 1 to the darker vision of Genesis 3—the so-called fall, or what I am

*calling the "problem." Instead of embracing God's
master plan for humanity and creation—what we
Franciscans still call the "Primacy of Christ"—Christians shrunk our image of both Jesus and Christ,
and our "Savior" became a mere Johnny-come-lately
"answer" to the problem of sin, a problem that we had
largely created ourselves. That's a very limited role
for Jesus. His death instead of his life was defined as
saving us! This is no small point. The shift in what we
valued often allowed us to avoid Jesus's actual life and
teaching because all we needed was the sacrificial event
of his death. Jesus became a mere mop-up exercise for
sin, and sin management has dominated the entire
religious story line and agenda to this day. This is no
exaggeration.*[40]

While I was always told that I was created in the image
of God, the emphasis was not on that but on sin being the
central theme. Like me, the concept of original goodness may
be counter to what you have believed in the past. Many evan-
gelical pastors only emphasize our sinful nature, insinuating
that we lost all likeness to God when sin entered the world. I
grew up believing that there was no goodness in me because
I was born into sin. It is no doubt confusing. We are often
pointed to Mark 10:17–18:

> *As Jesus started on his way, a man ran up to him and
> fell on his knees before him. "Good teacher," he asked,
> "what must I do to inherit eternal life?"*

"Why do you call me good?" Jesus answered. "No one is good—except God alone."

Billy Graham stated, "The word 'good' in the language of Scripture literally means 'to be like God,' because He alone is the One who is perfectly good."[41] Perhaps, Jesus is reminding this man that God is the only one who is perfect; we don't know exactly, but we do know that we are created in the image of God, and because of the fall in Genesis 3, we are also born with a sinful nature. Rohr agrees and acknowledges that both of these coexist. He wrote, "Just as goodness is inherent and shared, so it seems with evil."[42]

God created each one of us in His image, and yet we are sinners. We live in tension between our goodness and our sinfulness. We are participants in the war between good and evil. As Christians, we are image bearers who have repented from sin. We are to reflect God's goodness to the world. Paul writes in Ephesians 2:8–9, "For it is by grace you have been saved, through faith—and this is not from yourselves, it is the gift of God—not by works, so that no one can boast." God's grace is sufficient—I don't mean this flippantly, but thank God! God's grace is given to me freely. And, believer or not, God's grace is given to you. You possess the image of God, and His empowering Spirit enables you, as a sinner, to be good. Romans 3:23–24: "For all have sinned and fall short of the glory of God, and all are justified freely by his grace through the redemption that came by Christ Jesus."

Toxicity in the Workplace

The workplace often lacks goodness. It definitely isn't immune to evil. Open up your business news on any given day, and you will probably see corruption, violence, scandals, and discrimination. Evil is running rampant in corporations across the world. We know that evil will ultimately not win. We know that goodness will prevail, but we need to help that along; as Trillia Newbell says, "We need to overthrow the culture with good."[43] This requires that we are not just good; we are anti-evil, anti-corruption, and anti-workplace-toxicity.

Two years after the COVID pandemic began, the corporate world experienced what is now being called the great resignation. Workers left their jobs in record numbers, and Mark Perna says toxic work culture is the number one factor driving people to resign. In an article published in *Forbes* magazine, Perna stated:

> *According to MIT Sloan's recent study, toxic work culture is the number-one reason people cite for leaving their jobs. Organic marketing platform Conductor analyzed Google search volume and found that searches for "toxic work environment quiz" increased 700% in April alone. Conductor also found that "HIPAA violations in the workplace" searches increased 350%, "workplace mobbing" searches increased 190%, and "top workplaces 2022" searches increased 500%."* [44]

Perform a Google search for a toxic work environment, and I promise you will find hundreds of differing descriptions. People ranging from anyone who has ever had a job to workplace authorities like Adam Grant and Simon Sinek write articles about toxic work environments. One CNN article quoted Dr. Sara Fuller, who stated, "It's any workplace that makes you feel uncomfortable[45]." Others describe bullying and harassment as top indicators. In a Jessica Stillman article for *Inc Magazine*, she wrote, "Some of the confusion around what exactly makes for a toxic culture, according to VC and blogger Hunter Walk, is that a lot of us use the term 'toxic' in a loose way to mean simply a culture that doesn't appeal to us personally."[46]

I would contend that toxicity in the workplace occurs when there is a lack of goodness and destructive behaviors are prevalent. Some of these systemic behaviors are:

1. Lack of trust between leader and employee or within teams. This can look like micromanagement, a constant feeling you need to "cya," or being disrespected.

2. Being overworked. This equates to a distorted life balance when there is no opportunity for sabbath. Feeling like you have to check your email even during vacation for fear of missing something.

3. When gossip runs rampant. Hearing coworkers talk about others or participating in this type of gossip.

4. Hot-tempered leaders and coworkers: This can appear as an underlying lack of peace or can be explosive, angry behavior. Often, this leads to bullying and a culture of fear.

5. Performance expectations are not reasonable: When the demands that are placed on you are not possible, or there is too much beyond your control. This is a cutthroat environment where success is unattainable.

Other factors that can lead to toxicity include lack of transparency or fair and equitable compensation within your organization. By setting boundaries and practicing self-care, you can reduce the effects of the toxic environment on yourself. Sometimes that may be all the energy we have, but overall we want to be anti-evil, which means we want to take action that would reduce the toxicity for all.

Human-Centric Leadership Matters

The 2018 wildfire season was the most deadly and destructive on record in California, with over 7,500 fires burning over 1,670,000 acres. The CEO of our company had to evacuate his home, and with the state literally on fire, it was necessary to set up new equipment for him immediately. I was the leader closest to his temporary location, and our CIO dispatched me to help him. I'll be honest: I was nervous. I didn't typically support Mr. Dean, and I wanted to make a good impression. I rang the doorbell, and his daughter answered the door. She warmly welcomed me into her home and called out to her dad. Lloyd Dean came into the room, greeted me, and thanked me profusely for being there.

While I set up his equipment, he stayed in the room and chatted with me. He asked me what I thought about our company, Dignity Health, and asked about my thoughts on our upcoming merger. He took an interest in my family, inquiring about my kids and whether my travel schedule made my home life challenging. Before I left, he introduced me to his wife and thanked me again for taking time out of my Saturday to assist him. He showed real gratitude for my efforts.

Years later, I ran into Lloyd and his daughter on a plane. He approached me, and both remembered how I had shown up to help him a few years before. Demonstrating genuine gratitude for others and remembering those who have shown up for you, even years later, that, my friends, is goodness.

Several years ago, I experienced a leadership change at the top of my department. That leadership change resulted in the difference between a good culture and a toxic one. What a difference it was—trust versus no trust, life balance versus no life balance, psychological safety versus fear. Our reputation as one of Computer World's Best Places to Work was flipped overnight.

Some people lived every day in fear of losing their jobs. Many people felt that their worth was devalued. Consequently, we witnessed a decline in our once high standards of excellence, as we shifted to a mentality of just getting things done. We collectively made more mistakes, experienced a decline in customer service, and lost valuable employees. Good people left, and they followed good leaders to new jobs in new companies.

Leaders must recognize their power and use it for good. Get to know your employees, ask them how to make the culture better, be vulnerable, honest, and willing to change.

Employees must recognize that leaders aren't perfect. We should give grace to our leaders, and if there is toxicity in the environment, tell them. If it's toxic leadership, report it to HR. Encourage those around you, demonstrate acts of kindness to your coworkers, build a network of people you can trust, and be a light in the darkness.

Systemic Injustices

Ascension Health, based in St. Louis, Missouri, operates facilities throughout the United States. As a system, they took a stance on diversity and inclusion and created a framework for justice known as ABIDE. It stands for appreciation, belongingness, inclusivity, diversity, and equity. Their President and CEO Joseph Impicciche stated:

> *We have a shared responsibility and accountability, as individuals and as a ministry, to lead and model the changes we wish to see in our communities of valuing inclusion, justice and equity for all. This will not be an easy journey, but it is one we must take together. We must all ensure that individuals are treated justly and respectfully with equal access to opportunities and resources. We must also provide an inclusive culture where our associates feel valued, appreciated and welcome to contribute fully to Ascension's success and mission as they become agents for positive change in their communities.[47]*

When organizations put their stake in the ground, they become known for what they are for, and at Ascension Health it is very clear they are for justice.

We embody goodness when we are advocates for reconciliation and justice. Derek Vreeland wrote, "Weakness and vulnerability in the way of the cross does not look like silence in the light of injustice. Rather, it resembles an active resistance to striking back when we are stricken down and resisting the infliction of pain on the one who hurt us so deeply."[48] This anti-retaliatory sentiment was known by the first disciples commissioned by Jesus. In the *Unarmed Empire*, Reverend Sean Palmer states, "Jesus sends his first disciples out like lambs among wolves, armed only with vulnerability. The risk of vulnerability is the way of the cross."[49]

It's disheartening to hear people denying the existence of systemic injustices. I'll admit, at one time, I didn't believe systemic racism was real. I thought it was an excuse. My initial belief was that it was granting collective passes to groups of people, but I was mistaken. My views didn't change overnight, but they did change, and ultimately, I came to believe that systemic racism is one of the true evils in this world. How did I holistically change my view? I prayed, and I started researching.

Rather than taking a posture of condemnation, I took one of genuine curiosity. I started reading and asking questions. I read personal stories and history books. I looked at events from a different perspective. Seeking guidance, I prayed and asked God to reveal where I was wrong. But mostly, I talked with people affected by these systems. Ultimately, my views changed, and I asked God to help me continue learning and to use me as a reconciler. If you are like I was, denying these injustices exist, I would like to ask you a couple of questions. (1) Have you done your homework? (2) Have you talked with someone different than you about how race has impacted them? (3) Have you earnestly prayed and asked God to reveal His heart to you?

Robin J. Ely and David A. Thomas wrote "Getting Serious about Diversity" for *Harvard Business Review* 2022. In the article, Ely and Thomas implore their readers to create a safe space and culture that allows people the opportunity to take action. Learning about diversity and inclusion through a corporate program is a start, but not enough. They define four steps towards progress:

1. Build trust through conversation and relationships. Don't be afraid to reach out and be vulnerable to those that look different than you. It is through vulnerability and risk that one builds trust.
2. Actively work against discrimination. Read, seek to understand, and look for areas in your organization where systematic racism may be present. Lastly, address those areas, and take action on the items that are inhibiting equality and inclusion.
3. Embrace a wide range of styles and voices: In many companies, the dominant voice is an assertive white man. They say that people may think they are helpful when they instruct a no-nonsense white woman to be nicer or a

passionate Latina to dial it down, but all this communicates is how others see them, and it doesn't allow them to bring their full talents.

4. Make cultural differences a resource for learning: Encourage programs that dismantle systemic racism and promote discussions that learn about the various cultures in your workspace.[50]

In his book, *The Deeply Formed Life*, Pastor Rich Villodas introduces a habit called racial self-examination. This habit helps form us into people who don't look at the outward appearance. By asking ourselves a series of questions, we work towards identifying any subconscious biases and perspectives we may have. Pastor Rich's questions focus on our overall life, so I have restated these questions for us at work. Here are some questions you may want to ask yourself:

1. Is there a particular group or individual (gender, ethnicity, or race) that you subconsciously doubt their capability or commitment at work? Why?
2. Is there a group of people in the workplace you feel less comfortable collaborating with? Why?
3. When was the last time you sought mentorship, advice, or a working relationship with someone from a different cultural or gender background?
4. Who in the workplace do you most trust with critical responsibilities, and what qualities lead you to this choice?

5. Are there types of people (gender, background, or role) you find yourself avoiding in professional settings? Why?

6. What, if anything, do you notice within yourself when you see teams that are different from yours?

He closes this section by noting, "As we honestly respond to these questions, the internal scripts and messages that we have lived with can be met with alternative messages. This is deeply formed work. It's not easy, but as we identify the ways we've been deeply de-formed in our thinking toward others, we position ourselves to walk in greater freedom."[51]

Giving Back to Our Communities

Goodness exists when we give to others, expecting nothing in return. One way to create a culture of goodness is by giving back to our communities. Giving back is a behavior that spans across the fruit of the Spirit. It is rewarding and brings joy; it's loving, it's kind, certainly giving back is faithful, and it's also so very good. Developing a network of people within your workplace to give back to the community will benefit your coworkers and the people you serve.

Over the years our teams have given back in numerous ways. Whether it has been through established organizations like Feed My Starving Children or annual food drives. Giving back is the fruit of goodness. I recall times when we set up partnerships to donate computers to local schools, little leagues, and women's shelters. Many donated their time to philanthropic programs and galas. My colleague, Thaddeus, has a gift for being calm in crisis. His background in emergency medicine results in him always being a first responder on major incidents. Explore your gifts, figure out where you could use them to give back to your community and your workplace.

Let us not become weary in doing good, for at the proper time, we will reap a harvest if we do not give up. Therefore, as we have opportunity, let us do good to all people. The apostle Paul to the Galatians.

Tips and Biblical Encouragement

1. Goodness in the workplace looks like someone who does what they say they are going to do. Follow-through is so essential in the workplace. Following through on our commitments helps people see we can be trusted. When we fail, it creates doubt in the minds of those around us.

    Again, you have heard that it was said to the people long ago, "Do not break your oath, but fulfill to the Lord the vows you have made."

    — Matthew 5:33

2. We show goodness in the workplace when we are honest, even when there may be consequences. Sometimes being honest is challenging, whether it is confessing a mistake, delivering bad news, or telling someone something they don't want to hear. We must remain

truthful, even when the information may be unpopular or difficult to hear. I remember calling my leader one day and saying, "I made a five-million-dollar mistake." That was one of the most difficult phone calls I have ever made, but it was necessary.

Do not lie to each other, since you have taken off your old self with its practices.

— Colossians 3:9

3. Goodness is working hard and remembering that we work for God, not man. Have you ever experienced someone who just wasn't trying to help you? Think about a customer service experience where you knew the person could help you, but they were determined to do the bare minimum. It's frustrating; people notice, and frankly, it's not the way of God's goodness. Avis rental cars used to have a saying: "We try harder." I would contend that as Christians, we should try the hardest.

Whatever you do, work at it with all your heart, as working for the Lord, not for human masters, since you know that you will receive an inheritance from the Lord as a reward. It is the Lord Christ you are serving.

— Colossians 3:23–24

4. Taking responsibility. I once had a project manager working for me who kept reporting a green status on

his project despite everything going wrong, and we were way behind. Then I discovered that not only was he reporting the wrong status, but he was blaming the problems on someone else when it was clearly our problem. I remember calling the CIO, Deanna Wise, and telling her, "This project is in the red and it is completely our fault." I was terrified to do it, but she was patient, acknowledging her appreciation for the heads-up, and then giving me direction on how to proceed. (Leadership Matters)

He who conceals his sins does not prosper, but whoever confesses and renounces them finds mercy.

— Proverbs 28:13

5.   People that are good forgive just as our Father forgave us. In every aspect of our lives, people are going to let us down. Having a forgiving spirit is a quality of goodness.

Be kind and compassionate to one another, forgiving each other, just as in Christ God forgave you.

— Ephesians 4:32

6.   #6 Be a champion of inclusion. Jesus stripped away hierarchy and made us all one. Far too often, professing Christians demonstrate exclusivity rather than inclusivity. This is sinful, and as Christians, we must do everything we can to ensure equality and inclusion of people.

*There is neither Jew nor Gentile, neither slave nor
free, nor is there male and female, for you are all one
in Christ Jesus.*

— Galatians 3:28

Reflective Questions

1. How do we reflect God's goodness in our daily lives, especially in challenging situations?
2. How does our understanding of being created in God's image influence our actions and attitudes toward others?
3. How can we discern the right thing to do when faced with morally complex situations?
4. Consider Romans 12:21: *"Do not be overcome by evil, but overcome evil with good."* How can we actively work against toxicity and promote a culture of goodness in our workplaces?
5. What does it mean to be "salt and light" in our communities, and how does this relate to promoting goodness?
6. How can we practice forgiveness and extend grace to others, especially in situations where we encounter injustice?

CHAPTER 6

Gentleness

*I choose gentleness… Nothing is won by force. I choose
to be gentle. If I raise my voice, may it be only in
praise. If I clench my fist, may it be only in prayer. If I
make a demand, may it be only of myself.*

— Max Lucado[52]

Have you ever heard the expression, "He's like a bull in a china shop"? According to the Cambridge Dictionary, this means that someone is careless in how they move or behave.[53] To me, that sounds like the opposite of gentle. When I asked one of my friends if I was gentle, she responded by saying, "You are a force of nature." Eeek, that doesn't sound gentle at all! Months later I asked her to expand on this and she said, "You interrupt people, walk aggressively, loudly gulp your coffee, violently breathe when eating, type loud, and when you cook in the kitchen pots and pans are clanging noisily. Oh, and you are an aggressive driver." I was so glad I asked. We are never hanging out again, and I am considering deleting her phone number. In all seriousness, I have the ability to be gentle, but as my friend bluntly stated, I am not gentle by nature. It's fair to say gentleness doesn't come easy for me.

Gentleness: the act of being gentle, kind, not severe or rough, moderate. I can think of moments when I have been gentle, but I can think of more moments when I have lacked this fruit of the Spirit. It's a constant struggle for me, particularly with my children. I believe my lack of patience drives my lack of gentleness. Christopher Wright notes, "Gentleness is very close to patience. It's not surprising to find them both included in Paul's list of the fruit of the Spirit. What's the similarity and differences? Well, if patience is the ability to endure hostility and criticism without anger, then gentleness is the ability to endure such things without aggression."[54] I confess that I routinely need the Lord's intervention on this with me. For this reason, I feel pretty unqualified to write about this particular fruit of the Spirit. I pray that during this chapter, specifically, these words are birthed out of listening to the Spirit and that these words can resonate with you, the reader.

A few images come to mind when I think of gentleness. A father cradling a sleeping baby, Psalm 23, my daughter Sydney in the few moments she still wants to cuddle as a 16-year-old growing teenager, and my husband as he cared for his mother when she was dying of cancer. In those final days, I watched my husband carry her back and forth from the bathroom with a calm and gentle spirit I hadn't seen in him before. I watched him exhibit gentleness in the way he would bring the cup to her mouth to provide her with a sip of water. I watched him speak softly and be tender-hearted as he would attend to each of her needs. Over the years, I have learned that, contrary to what I had previously thought, gentleness is a show of strength. Gentleness is holy.

My greatest picture of gentleness, though, comes directly from Jesus. My parents have a sculpture in their home of Jesus with little children surrounding Him. It is an artistic depiction of Matthew 19:13–14:

> *Then people brought little children to Jesus for him to place his hands on them and pray for them. But the disciples rebuked them. Jesus said, "Let the little children come to me, and do not hinder them, for the kingdom of heaven belongs to such as these." When he had placed his hands on them, he went on from there.*

Jesus took the time to let the children come to him. As I think of that now, I am instantly remorseful for the way I tell my children to get out of my office—usually with a harsh tone when I am working. Guess what? Not only is that training my children not to be gentle, but the people I am interacting with on my Zoom calls sometimes see that. They see the not-so-gentle Kim Thomas, who is short-tempered with her children. I can only hope and pray that my two girls forgive me, for I have not done a great job of demonstrating gentleness to them. To those that have observed this, I would ask you to pray that I focus on being gentle, gentle like Jesus.

Gentleness at Work

Several years ago, one of my direct reports had just about enough of me. I lived in California, and my team was scattered across the western states. Most of the Information Technology team was in our data center building, which was in Phoenix,

Arizona. I often visited this location for meetings and to check in with the team. On one particular visit, Laura Martin, the corporate office manager who worked for me, looked at me exasperated and said, "You are like a tornado! You blow into town, issue a bunch of orders, and then leave." Whoa, that hurt, but it was honest; it was how she felt, and I have no doubt she felt that way because of my actions, because of my lack of gentleness.

We live in a non-gentle world, and we certainly don't consider gentleness a quality of corporate America or the working world in general. We are a harsh and polarized society, and more often than not, that extends to the workplace. How can we integrate gentleness amid a rough, complex, and angry world?

Gentleness is rare, and it stands out. Dwayne Paul is a strong and gentle leader and mentor. I worked alongside Dwayne for the better part of twenty years. In a complicated outsourcing agreement, he was my customer; as healthcare IT services delivery senior director, he was my leader, and most recently, a peer of mine as he led talent in our performance and effectiveness department. Dwayne would often get tapped by people for specific instances when we would need an analytical look at a contract, an expert operational eye, or a calming presence within our organization.

One such time, he was called into an unusual situation during the COVID-19 pandemic. We needed someone with the ability to have a calm and clear head to lead, represent us, and tie our IT teams together as we delivered service to our healthcare organization. Dwayne was that person; he established a framework and organized our many service lines so that we could provide help and make the complex as simple as possible for our teams and our caregivers. He led flawlessly; when we became unfocused, he calmly and gently would steer us back in the right direction. Dwayne's mild manner and his ability to navigate and embody calmness in the face of such unknown and sheer chaos set us up for success. With his leadership, the team built confidence and momentum. We were seemingly making the impossible happen by accomplishing more in days than we usually would in months. Our work would have been significantly more stressful without his calming, gentle guidance and presence.

As I mentally ran through the wonderful people I have worked with over the years, my thoughts paused on my executive support team. Providing technology support for executives is no easy task—it's a tough gig. Their demands are high, and the expectation for flawless performance is constant. Yet, as we all know, technology can be unpredictable. Through my experience in recruiting support personnel for our executives, one trait stands out above all: gentleness. Executives operate in a whirlwind of high-pressure situations, and what they value most is a calm and composed demeanor in their support team. The ability to speak softly and maintain composure in the face of chaos not only reassures the executive but also fosters a productive and harmonious working environment. I think of Trevor, Matt, Gerson, and William. Priscilla, Danny, Ian, and Michael. Rob, John, Mat, and Laura. These are some of the most gentle people I know. Their capacity to remain calm shows confidence and soothes those around them.

My friend Kelli Sue and I are wildly different and, at the same time, in some ways, we are very similar. Like me, I don't think gentleness would be a characteristic most people would use to describe her, but her capacity for gentleness is great. We have worked together off and on for almost ten years, and during that time, I have discovered that she is someone with whom my greatest thoughts and fears can be trusted. Some of my greatest laughs and cries have occurred with her; I think she would say the same in return. I recall a time when she was remarkably gentle with me, and it was ironically over FaceTime. Gentleness displayed through a handheld device with my friend hundreds of miles away. We all need people like this who are safe and gentle with our emotions and, above all, who see us and are empathetic and loving. God puts these individuals in our lives to mediate His gentleness. They don't take the place of Jesus, but they are on this earth as gifts to each of us.

Like Kelli Sue, my capacity for gentleness increases dramatically when someone is in need. I can't count the number of people or the number of times I have gently held space for someone who was hurting. Without a doubt, my gentleness shows up through empathy and presence.

There was something not right with one of my employees. He didn't sound like his usual self; he was getting his work done, but there was something off, something unsettling. I couldn't put my finger on it.

Despite leading a geographically dispersed team, I often feel guided to where I'm needed, a sense, an instinct that I attribute to the Holy Spirit. As I was going to bed one night, I told my husband I needed to be in Phoenix the next day. He asked me why, and I said I didn't know, but I knew I needed to be there. I woke up, booked a flight, and called the individual. I told him I would be there to take him to lunch.

Turns out, the individual had a lot going on. I discovered he was facing personal challenges and needed support. He needed a friend and a boss who would listen, understand, and lean in with advice. Was it my place to do that? Probably not; ask human resources, and they would likely say to give him the employee assistance hotline instead. By the way, I did offer that to him. If there are tangible employee benefits, use them. But what he really needed was support from someone who knew and loved him. He needed someone to gently come alongside him, place a hand on his shoulder, and say, "I am with you and I am for you." I reminded him of his value, his innate gifts, and reassured him of God's love without conditions. When I left him that day, I made it clear to him I would be there for him throughout the situation.

Laura's comment from over five years ago has stuck with me. When we receive feedback we might not like, we shouldn't dismiss it. We should use the feedback to make us better. I want to be known as a leader who is more like Dwayne and less like a tornado.

The Good and Gentle Shepherd

The shepherd is a symbol used throughout the Bible to illustrate protection, authority, caretaking, leadership, and all of God's people. While shepherds are less common today, in biblical times, shepherds held prevalent roles. Sheep had value as they provided clothing, milk, meat, and even materials for musical instruments. People entrusted shepherds with the care of their sheep, relying on them to feed, nurture, and protect the animals.

The first shepherd mentioned is Abel in Genesis 4, and the shepherd's profession is seen repeatedly from there:

- We see shepherds turned prophets.
- We see King David begin his work as a shepherd.
- We see shepherds make their way to celebrate Jesus.
- We see Jesus refer to Himself as the Good Shepherd.

In recalling Psalm 23 verses 2–3, Gerald Wilson says:

The shepherd leads his sheep in pleasant places full of all the necessities of life: green pastures of grass and quiet streams providing water for drinking. Those who have visited the undeveloped lands of the Bible will know just how unusual this picture is. At best, the land is a dry, rocky set of rolling hills covered with a sparse and tough grass. Water sources are few and often seasonal. Shepherds had to be ready to take their flocks on long migrations from one source of grazing and water to another. The psalmist paints a scene of abundant life in three descriptive statements—each speaking of the shepherd in the third person, the shepherd causes the sheep to lie down, makes them approach quiet waters carefully, and leads them

faithfully on the correct paths. All three images empha-
size the shepherd's role as provider.[55]

This image of the gentle shepherd providing his sheep
with water, food, and rest is stark. As Wilson reminds us, this
picture comes from a parched land, not the rolling hills of an
English countryside. The terrain here is harsh; water is scarce,
and the predators are vicious. As I ponder that kind of gentle
setting for the sheep, it's like an oasis of peace in the midst of a
turbulent world. It's a sacred space that the shepherd protects.
In the workplace, it's the sacred cubicle. It's the place where
you instantly feel safe and secure.

We all know people who make us feel inherently safe. They
gently communicate with us that we are out of harm's way in
their presence. These are the people I shed occasional tears
with. These are individuals who wrap their arms around me
when I am weak and let me know I am not alone. These are
the people who encourage me, even in the harsh terrain of
the corporate environment. These people show up. They can
lend an ear or a helping hand and help us through the times
when the tension is high and our capacity is low. Gentleness
in the workplace is an expression of God's love and the Spirit's
empowering presence.

My friends, may we look to Jesus as our Good Shepherd?
He's not simply our model; He is our Savior. When we are
weak and burdened from the lack of gentleness we encounter,
let us remember Matthew 11 verses 28–30, where Jesus tells
us, "Come to me, all you who are weary and burdened, and I
will give you rest. Take my yoke upon you and learn from me,
for I am gentle and humble in heart, and you will find rest for

your souls. For my yoke is easy and my burden is light." Similar to kindness, showing gentleness to others is challenging when we fail to be gentle with ourselves. When we learn to be gentle with ourselves, we can, in turn, be gentle with others.

I love how Matthew Dickerson describes the way we cultivate the virtues of kindness and gentleness. He says:

> *They come from the work of the Holy Spirit in our lives. As noted, they won't come from imitating the heroes of our culture. They also won't come from mere self-effort. No self-empowered striving will suddenly make us gentle against the worldly current and culture of harshness. We need the Holy Spirit to be working within us. We need to submit to the Spirit's work and participate in that work. One simple way to start would be to pray that the Spirit will help us be kinder and more gentle—acknowledging that we can't do it on our own and inviting the Spirit to do that work within us. Perhaps we even need to start by asking the Spirit to help us desire to be gentle.*[56]

Blessed Are the Meek

At the beginning of Matthew 5, Jesus goes through a list of people He calls blessed. Blessed are the meek, for they will inherit the earth. Meekness, often being meek, is thought of as being weak, shy, or mousy, but meekness is a sign of strength and humility. Let's look at what a couple of scholars have to say about meekness.

Thomas Aquinas was a medieval theologian who described meekness this way: "Meekness is a gentleness that restrains us from anger or from expressing our anger easily."[57]

Scot McKnight, one of the world's top scholars on New Testament theology, describes it this way: "The meek are those who suffer and who have been humbled, and yet they do not seek revenge but God's glory and the welfare of others. In other words, they lovingly trust God and hope in God's timing and God's justice."[58]

Scholar John Stott says, "Meekness is a true view of oneself expressed in attitude and conduct with respect to others. This makes us gentle, humble, sensitive, and patient in all our dealings with others."[59]

There is perhaps no more significant evidence that I am not in sync with God than when I lack gentleness. It's the first fruit (followed by patience) where I can tell (and so can others) that I am out of sorts. This type of out-of-sorts behavior is an indication that I have drifted into sinfulness. And it aligns with what John Wesley says about meekness:

> *It keeps clear of every extreme, whether in excess or defect. It does not destroy but balance the affections, which the God of nature never designed, should be rooted out by grace, but only brought and kept under due regulations. It poises the mind aright. It holds an even scale, with regard to anger, and sorrow, and fear; preserving the mean in every circumstance of life, and not declining either to the right hand or the left.[60]*

We looked at four different scholars with four slightly different interpretations of meekness. Meekness is tricky. That's why it is so often misunderstood. People don't know what to think about meekness. As I read commentaries and different views of meekness, I too was stumped. I remember hearing my onetime pastor, Reverend Leach, say that meekness was a strength, not a weakness. It was the first time I had heard it that way. As Thomas Aquinas describes it as slow to anger, Scot McKnight describes it as humble, John Stott describes it as gentle, and then John Wesley says it's about lacking extremism. I see it as anything but weak. For just a minute, think about the polarization in our world today.

- Meekness is not extreme left or extreme right.
- Meekness is not Republican or Democrat.
- Meekness is not about always being right or wrong.
- Meekness is not about power or weakness.
- Meekness is about resolution.
- Meekness is about apologizing when we are wrong.
- Meekness is about being gentle.
- Meekness is about controlling one's strength.
- Meekness is about trusting God instead of ourselves.
- Meekness is about following God, no matter what.

Today, I argued with my leader about something impactful for our team. While we agreed to disagree, I apologized for my tone. If I had taken a posture of humility and listened longer rather than one of pride, perhaps we would have come to a more favorable ending. Instead, arrogance and a lack of gentleness came through.

At the beginning of this chapter, I confessed I didn't feel qualified to write it. I have struggled with this chapter more than any other combined. I texted a friend yesterday:

Me: *I'm struggling to write about gentleness*

Friend: *Because you aren't gentle? (Insert laughing emoji.)*

Me: *Right, that's it.*

Tips and Biblical Encouragement

So, how do we embody gentleness if it doesn't come naturally to us? How do we show gentleness to others?

1. Speak kindly. This doesn't mean speaking quietly. It means not being harsh. It means watching our tone. Too often, it is not what we say, but how we say it.

   A gentle answer turns away wrath, but a harsh word stirs up anger.

   — Proverbs 15:1

2.   Be reasonable. There is no place for unreasonableness
      in the workplace. If you are being unreasonable, check
      yourself. It's not gentle, and it certainly isn't Christ-like.

Let your gentleness be evident to all. The Lord is near.
                                    — Philippians 4:5

3.   Refrain from being quick to anger. I recall a time when
      someone who worked for me came to me and said that
      they couldn't work with a couple of particular leaders. It
      didn't seem to matter the scenario; this leader was quick
      to anger. Often, they wouldn't let the team members
      explain before they were interjecting with rage. The
      team was done.

My dear brothers and sisters, take note of this:
Everyone should be quick to listen, slow to speak and
slow to become angry.
                                    — James 1:9

4.   Be tenderhearted. Some of my greatest cries out to
      God revolve around those I love with hardened hearts.
      I pray for God to chisel away hardened hearts so they
      become tender and childlike. This is often seen through
      empathy. God, show us how to put ourselves in the
      shoes of the other and be empathetic. May we hurt
      when others hurt, grieve when others grieve, and lean
      in with an empathetic heart to those we encounter.

Finally, all of you should be of one mind. Sympathize with each other. Love each other as brothers and sisters. Be tender-hearted and keep a humble attitude.

— 1 Peter 3:8 (NLT)

5. Gentleness requires giving the benefit of the doubt. A gentle response does not make assumptions but seeks to understand. When we come to conclusions on our own, we do a disservice to those we are working with and erode trust.

Don't jump to conclusions, there may be a perfectly good explanation for what you just saw.

— Proverbs 25:8

6. #5 Smile. A genuine smile defuses. Sometimes, my kids ask me what is wrong because my face shows a frown or anger. I have simply been making a concerted effort to smile. It's a sign of being welcome and gentle.

Strength and dignity are her clothing, and she smiles at the future.

— Proverbs 31:25

Reflective Questions

1. How can I emulate the gentleness of Jesus in my daily interactions, particularly with those closest to me?

2. How can a gentle response in challenging situations demonstrate the love and patience of God?

3. Consider how a gentle and loving demeanor can be an effective witness for Jesus in fulfilling the Great Commission.

4. How can I balance assertiveness and gentleness in the workplace, ensuring that my attitude reflects Christ-like humility?

5. When faced with anger or frustration, how can I choose to respond with patience and gentleness rather than aggression?

6. What practical steps can I take to foster a more gentle spirit, even when it doesn't come naturally to me?

7. How can I be more gentle and forgiving toward myself, acknowledging my imperfections and relying on God's grace?

CHAPTER 7

Self-Control

Discipline yourself to do the things you need to do when you need to do them, and the day will come when you will be able to do the things you want to do when you want to do them.

— Zig Ziglar[61]

When I think of self-control, the first thing that comes to mind is temptation. Although our temptations may differ, we are all too familiar with the concept. It may be food, shopping, apathy, sex, laziness, or something else. Whatever it is, temptation has been at your door.

Open up the Bible, and you won't have to wait long for temptation to rear its ugly head. In Genesis 3:1–6, we see the first example of temptation when Eve commits the Bible's first sin, otherwise known as the Fall.

The Bible says:

Now the serpent was more crafty than any of the wild animals the Lord God had made. He said to the woman, "Did God really say, 'You must not eat from any tree in the garden'?"

The woman said to the serpent, "We may eat fruit from the trees in the garden, but God did say, 'You must not eat fruit from the tree that is in the middle of the garden, and you must not touch it, or you will die.'"

"You will not certainly die," the serpent said to the woman. "For God knows that when you eat from it your eyes will be opened, and you will be like God, knowing good and evil."

When the woman saw that the fruit of the tree was good for food and pleasing to the eye, and also desirable for gaining wisdom, she took some and ate it. She also gave some to her husband, who was with her, and he ate it."

Three chapters into the Bible, the first two humans indulge in temptation, bringing about the Fall of humanity and the broken world we live in today. There is no doubt self-control is a pretty big deal to God.

Self-Control at Work

Self-control may look different from what you would expect. How does self-control play into our work life? Is it working hard, trying to stay clear of office gossip, and general rule following? It's much more than that. At first, I thought this fruit was easier than some of the others, but when I dug into it, I realized I was wrong. For me, self-control is one of the hardest.

What if when we thought about self-control it wasn't just the big things like controlling our tempers or avoiding inappropriate office relationships? What if self-control included the little things, such as regularly being on time for meetings? I once knew someone who was constantly running late. It was becoming a big problem in the office. Rather than leaving for work ten minutes earlier, the person resorted to speeding and occasionally running traffic lights to make it to meetings on time.

I have broken up self-control at work into five major themes so we can properly unpack it.

(1) Communication and Interactions with Others

Actively listen and be attentive to others.

Paying attention when people are talking is respectful. From time to time, I'm sure most of us have been guilty of failing to listen well. As one who has a lot going on, I can easily become distracted. How many times have I had to ask for something to be repeated because I was multitasking and not listening to the conversation? Countless. Not only is failing to listen well irritating, but it shows a disregard for the time of those around you.

There was a period a few years ago when I was really struggling with this. I had to do something drastic to stop myself from multitasking on my phone. I installed a random app called "Forest." Forest is a simulation app in which you create a forest. When you plant something, it will die if you pick up your phone and leave the app before the timer goes off. Timers are customizable so I can set a timer for focused work, length of a meeting, or anything else I want. Now, if I get distracted and pick up my phone, I am reminded immediately to put it back down. As ridiculous as this may sound, it helped me retrain my brain to minimize distractions.

Use a calm and respectful tone when communicating.

At times, it can take every bit of our patience and kindness to turn the other cheek and respond respectfully. When we do, we subvert culture and people notice. People wonder how you could maintain your composure. Whether it's responding to an unfair email, a personal attack, or unwarranted criticism, in these times, the need for self-control is clear. It's also an opportunity for people to see the power of the spirit working in and through you. Responding with self-control doesn't mean being a doormat; it simply means responding thoughtfully and respectfully to the situation.

Be wise when speaking, don't interrupt, and wait your turn.

Have you ever been in a meeting with someone who dominates and interjects throughout the entire conversation? This behavior is an obvious demonstration of a lack of self-awareness and self-control. By monopolizing discussions and disregarding the input of others, they exhibit an inability to regulate their impulses and show respect for their colleagues. It stifles collaboration and diminishes the contributions of others. In a few of these situations, I have found myself compelled to apologize on behalf of the organization for time wasted in unproductive meetings.

(2) Managing Your Time and Productivity

Establish a reputation as a doer.

Avoid procrastination and jump on your work. My team at Mercy San Juan Hospital in Sacramento, California, was known for their commitment to customer service. Dustin Karnesky tells the story of one of their tactics to avoid procrastination and be disciplined in their work. Dustin wrote:

> *Early in my career in Healthcare IT, I was part of a team that kept track each day of how many service tickets we could close as a team. We had an idea to post a calendar in the office and circle each day that we could get our ticket queue to 0. The competition that followed over the next several years was amazing! We would stalk the queue each day, racing to complete our tickets. If someone had a problem they were bogged down on, the team would jump in and do whatever they could to help so that we could Sharpie in a proud circle around that date on the calendar. Not only did we see our team metrics improve, but our customers reaped the benefits of a team that was hustling to get each of their problems solved.[62]*

I remember every one of my visits to this team, and I recall how proud they were to show me their calendar and all the dates circled. I was always so proud of their work. I still am.

Mindfully spend your time.

I have known a few colleagues who habitually engage in excessive personal conversations and distractions during work hours. I am not referring to the occasional lengthy catchup with an office friend but the act of wandering the office, going from cube to cube, gossiping and carrying on long personal conversations. These behaviors kill workplace productivity. It's important to be mindful of your time as well as respect the time of others.

Set realistic goals and timelines.

One way I struggle with self-control is by being overly optimistic about what I can accomplish and then missing a deadline. I have always pushed back to ensure the team didn't receive unrealistic goals, but personally, I have had to force myself to get better at this. By evaluating the requirements of incoming requests immediately, this has resulted in me providing more accurate time estimations for work that I need to complete.

(3) Keep Your Emotions Regulated and in Check

Manage stress and avoid emotional outbursts.

We all get stressed, but how we deal with it in the workplace can make or break us and our witness in this world. I recall having a bad day and on a call with my direct reports, frustrated, I blurted out several curse words. One of them who had worked for me for years called me afterwards and said, "What is going on? Are you okay? I can't believe Kim Thomas just said that. That was the first time I heard you use a curse word." At that moment, I realized that my losing self-control was clear to the team. Using inappropriate language may be common in the business world, but it doesn't reflect the God we follow or show maturity.

Avoid impulsive decision making.

I was once responsible for a team that made large changes to the computing environment. These changes had a positive impact on device stability, but we always had to conduct thorough testing before implementing them. I recall one occasion when the team didn't take the time to test enough, and when rolling out the product, it broke thousands of devices from communicating. The team tried to fix it quickly so that nobody would notice, but their efforts didn't work. By the time they paused and called for help, they had made the situation more complicated, which resulted in more downtime for the customers. These types of incidents occur when we are quick to cover up a situation and fail to slow down and discern the proper approach.

Recognize emotional triggers and develop strategies for coping with them.

We all have things that challenge our ability to be emotionally self-controlled. An emotional trigger for me is when I am in conflict with someone I care deeply for. My mom, my sisters, and close friends are at the top of this list. While rare, when things aren't right, I get really emotional and want it resolved. It obsessively occupies my thoughts, and it's hard for me to self-regulate. I have learned that the best strategy for me is to take a few hours off work and go for a prayer walk, letting my tears (all of them) fall while I talk it out with God. I find taking the time off is better for me, my team, and my witness.

(4) Manage Your Behaviors and Code of Conduct

Be ambitious and godly.

Ambitious individuals typically possess discipline, courage, and eagerness. They show commitment to what they are pursuing and strive for greatness, but ambition without godliness can quickly turn negative. I have an overly ambitious friend who works in sales. She does well for herself and her family, but when we catch up, she often talks about how she is always strategizing and playing the game to win. While I applaud strategizing, the examples she uses represent a fake persona. Instead of being real with her customers, she puts on an act involving trickery and a false self to win the sale. She will use any means necessary to make herself look good. She proclaims she is Christ-like, but it's hard for me to see Jesus in her when she is showing that she is out for herself.

Foster collaboration, not competition, to get ahead.

Competition can be obvious or stealthy. Dustin told me about an issue he experienced. He said, "We had an issue one morning that affected the entire organization. The issue was highly visible and was caused by a simple mistake by an engineer. During the triage call, a high-level VP dropped in hot, aggressively interrogating everyone on the call, demanding to know who caused the issue. The entire engineering team deflected the questioning, protecting their teammate. They calmly communicated that they were aware of the cause and stayed focused on resolving the problem. It would have been easy to throw a colleague under the bus in front of influential people, but the team wasn't competing. They stayed focused on the task at hand and didn't worry about placing blame."[63]

Do not take part in discord.

Individuals who incite discord within a community often become the epicenter of turmoil. I once collaborated with a leader who had a penchant for concocting crises as a smokescreen to divert attention from problems within his own department. He habitually interfered with the interpersonal dynamics of team members, sowing seeds of unrest and misunderstanding. This behavior not only led to a palpable sense of unease among staff but also eroded the foundation of trust that is crucial for a cohesive team environment. As a result, the workplace became fraught with suspicion, where colleagues were wary of each other's motives, and the overall morale suffered. This toxic atmosphere stifled collaboration and innovation, ultimately hampering the organization's ability to function effectively. The ripple effects of such actions underscore the importance of fostering unity rather than division.

(5) Personal Habits and Health

Take regular breaks at work.

We have talked about the importance of sabbath in other chapters, but it's also important to include rest in your workday. Part of self-control is not overworking. While God put us on the earth for work, He also put us here for rest.

Ask for help when you need it.

We don't have to know all the answers for everything. Sometimes we can lack self-control by not asking for help. We may think we are going at everything alone, but God has given us resources to help us. Whether it be a colleague, parent, friend, or even helpline, when we need assistance, we need to reach out for help.

Self-Control and Sin

When you think about it, most, if not all, of our sins could be chalked up to a lack of self-control. Proverbs 6:16–19 states, "There are six things the Lord hates, seven that are detestable to him: haughty eyes, a lying tongue, hands that shed innocent blood, a heart that devises wicked schemes, feet that are quick to rush into evil, a false witness who pours out lies and a man who stirs up dissension among brothers." You may notice a common denominator in these seven sins. These sins can significantly impact others; these sins hurt other people, and because of that, we see the word: detestable. In the tables below, we see the seven sins accompanied by some workplace examples:

Trust erosion is common in the workplace, whether telling half-truths, inappropriately exaggerating, or intentionally minimizing a situation. It's the subtle lies we are more likely to fall prey to. Those little lies that we justify to ourselves because they don't really matter. Or do they?

- "Oh, I'm sorry. I could have sworn I sent you that status report" (when I haven't started it yet).
- "The impact of the error was small" (when it was more than minimal).

- "Your zoom broke up for a minute, can you repeat that?" (when I wasn't paying attention).
- "I haven't been able to get a hold of them" (when I haven't tried).
- "I apologize for being late, an urgent matter needed my attention" (when I lost track of time).
- "No, I haven't talked to the client yet, but I left a message" (before hurrying to leave a message).

Surely, some of these resonate with you. What are the "little" lies you tell?

A heart that devises wicked schemes does not have the best interest of everyone or the organization in mind. They are plotting and scheming. One-upping people is common, and they put their desires ahead of the needs of others.

I once became aware of someone who was stealing from the company. I was really upset about the situation, and when a direct report and I started investigating, we were absolutely sickened. The thief had quite the racket going, and neither of us could believe it had happened under our noses. The scheming that had taken place dumbfounded us.

Feet that are quick to rush into evil. This person lacks wisdom, discernment, and self-control. The absence of these three qualities is a recipe for sinful and destructive behavior.

A false witness who pours out lies. The characteristic of the false witness is deception. Facts are distorted and twisted, situations are exaggerated, and blame is often assigned to others. The false witness is an expert in deflection and sometimes can be so masterful at deceit that it's difficult to spot.

Occasionally, I adopt a Pollyanna perspective. If I was giving out an award for "least likely to be let go," it would have been this leader. Bad things just don't happen to good people. Yet, in May 2020, the company unexpectedly laid off a well-regarded colleague of mine from her pivotal role in healthcare information technology. Renowned for her wisdom, judiciousness, and winsomeness, she had recently led her team to implement virtual care solutions and various other initiatives successfully amidst the pandemic. She directed her attention towards using her sphere of influence to improve things for people, whether patients, colleagues, or anyone else she encountered.

Her departure sent shockwaves throughout the organization, as many saw her as the very heart and essence of the company. She embodied its values and mission with unparalleled dedication. The news of her departure left her team in utter disbelief, and the sense of loss continues to resonate, even four years later. The narrative provided to the teams proved to be inaccurate. Disinformation sparked widespread speculation and ultimately led to a severe deterioration of the organization's culture. In a matter of days, the absence of her and the misleading communication surrounding it decimated the trust and camaraderie painstakingly built over years, highlighting the profound impact.

It's safe to say that temptation exists around each of these sins. Some of these may be more of a temptation than others. Lying is more of a temptation to me than haughty eyes. You would never catch me telling a big, bold lie, but if I am honest, you might see me exaggerating a situation or making something look like I was farther along on an assignment than

I actually was. In the past, I have exaggerated work effort because I knew team members were behind and just needed a breather or even a little less pressure. Maybe I had good intentions, but I was still misrepresenting the time to completion. James E. Faust once said, "Honesty is more than not lying. It is truth-telling, truth speaking, truth living, and truth loving."[64]

What does self-control actually look like in the workplace?

- Self-control is exercising discipline and avoiding distractions while working.
- Self-control is not engaging in office gossip.
- Self-control is resting on the Sabbath day.
- Self-control is showing restraint with your words when you are angry.
- Self-control is not sending that angry email.
- Self-control is listening before speaking.
- Self-control is prioritizing what you need to do rather than what you want to do.
- Self-control is embodying the fruit of the Spirit in everything you do.
- Self-control is not being the first to always speak out in a meeting.
- Self-control is praying through difficult situations and responding rather than reacting.

Joshua Nangle said:

> *As Christians, the inability to control what we say can bring disunity in the body of Christ, and this is the very thing Jesus prayed against in John 17:11. In the*

workplace, a loose tongue can push colleagues apart, which disrupts the efficiency of our work. Self-control allows us to remain on task, but a lack of control causes our mission to drift. We have all seen and heard of countless examples where the mission of a business, sports team, or ministry was derailed because of a lack of self-control among its members. As Christians, we are called to control our thoughts, words, and deeds, and this is accomplished when we invite the Spirit's presence into our daily lives.[65]

Managing Our Thoughts

Managing thoughts is a key to self-control. Think about a time when your thoughts got the better of you. I was once preparing a presentation for a brand-new executive. I heard this individual was demanding and hard to impress. A colleague said the executive had spent their meeting poking holes into his plan. Anxiety consumed me; I had dreamt up a worst-case scenario in my mind. When I entered the room to present, my thoughts were jumbled and I didn't do well. Afterward, I realized I had allowed myself to get so intimidated and rattled that it shook my confidence to the core. My negative thoughts got the better of me.

Do you realize your thoughts matter to God? Philippians 4:8 says, "Finally, brothers and sisters, whatever is true, whatever is noble, whatever is right, whatever is pure, whatever is lovely, whatever is admirable—if anything is excellent or praiseworthy—think about such things." Paul tells us here that our thoughts should be consumed with good things. This can be a real struggle for me. Negative self-talk can run rampant in my mind. I am not good enough. I am not smart enough. In meetings, I am not quick enough on my feet. I am too easygoing. I am too chaotic. I am too predictable. I am also a master at jumping to conclusions. Why haven't I heard from my boss? Is she mad at me? What did I do wrong? Last week, I was on the phone with a colleague who had those exact thoughts. It was easy for me to tell him not to worry, that she was busy, but he was convinced he had done something wrong, and she was now avoiding him.

Spiraling thoughts can cause action paralysis or lead to impulsive and irrational behavior. Mastering them is not easy, but there are strategies we can use when we notice our thoughts getting out of control.

Here are a few strategies you can try:

- First, I suggest slowing down and turning your thoughts to the Spirit of the living God. In the peace chapter, we discussed breath prayers. Breath prayers are a vital tool I use when my thoughts are spiraling.
- Second, consider what you would say to a friend if they shared these spiraling thoughts with you. Then take your own advice.
- Third, change your environment. Go for a walk, or call a friend.

Taking that shortcut at work can seem so easy. Shortcuts those moments when we withhold pertinent information or don't follow the cumbersome policy, knowing there could be consequences to others. It might make the situation more manageable, but that doesn't mean it's right. As a leader, I often have to discern whether taking a shortcut is the right thing to do or the wrong thing to do. The awe-inspiring part of the Holy Spirit is that if I am listening, I generally know quickly whether that shortcut is right or wrong. If it doesn't feel right, it's always wrong. Every time I have taken a shortcut that didn't feel right, it has come back to bite me, or I have had to reconcile the situation—every single time.

If we are breathing, walking, and running by the power of the Spirit, we can resist instant gratification, choose discipline, and exercise self-control. You see, the Spirit knows, and the Spirit will lead you towards the right decision. Sometimes, that decision may be difficult, for we know that living as a Christian in this world is not easy. Jesus himself tells us this: He says in John 16:33, "In this world you will have trouble," but He follows that up with one of the most hopeful statements in the Bible. He says, "But take heart! I have overcome the world." Those two lines give us a reason to press on! Those two lines send shivers down my spine! Jesus, our redeemer, has overcome the world!

I was sitting with a friend today who described the consequences she had given her six-year-old daughter. Over the weekend, her daughter had acted out at a birthday party. It just so happened the next day was another birthday party. My friend made her daughter stay home from the second party. As a result, the child threw a tantrum, and my friend told me, "It's easier to let her go to the party, but our jobs as parents don't mean taking the easy way." I wish I were better at this. I am praying for discipline in this area of my life. Self-control is usually the more challenging path. Whether in self-managing, parenting, or our sacred cubicle of work. It's not taking the path of least resistance; it's taking the right way, no matter the cost.

Tips and Biblical Encouragement

How can we exemplify self-control in our workplace?

1. Managing our thoughts.

    Set your minds on things above, not on earthly things.
    — Colossians 3:2

2. Self-control means we control our tongue. We listen before speaking, and we don't lash out in frustration.

    My dear brothers and sisters, take note of this: Everyone should be quick to listen, slow to speak, and slow to become angry.
    — James 1:9

3. We are self-disciplined people. We manage our responsibilities even if we would instead do other things.

    For the Spirit God gave us does not make us timid, but gives us power, love and self-discipline.
    — 2 Timothy 1:7

4.   Remember that the Spirit provides us with a way out of temptations. When confronted with temptations, the Spirit is not far away but present with us. Consciously and deliberately, look to the Spirit for guidance. Get started by pausing for a sacred moment of prayer.

No temptation has overtaken you except what is common to mankind. And God is faithful; he will not let you be tempted beyond what you can bear. But when you are tempted, he will also provide a way out so that you can endure it.

— 1 Corinthians 10:13

Reflective Questions

1.   How does the story of Eve's temptation in Genesis 3:1–6 resonate with the temptations you face today? How can you apply the lessons from this story to resist temptations in your own life?
2.   In what ways can exercising self-control at work be a witness to others of your faith and the presence of the Holy Spirit in your life?
3.   Reflect on a recent situation where you struggled with self-control in your communication or interactions at work. How could you have handled it differently in a way that reflects Christ's love?

4. In what ways can ambition without godliness lead to negative outcomes in the workplace? How can you ensure that your ambition aligns with godly principles?

5. Reflect on how you manage your thoughts, especially during challenging times. How can Philippians 4:8 guide you in maintaining a positive and godly mindset?

6. How does practicing self-control in small, everyday decisions at work reflect your commitment to following Jesus?

CHAPTER 8
Faithfulness

*Continue to be faithful to our God because our God
is faithful to us. If you stay faithful in your pursuit of
God and learn to embrace your place, His work in and
through you will be unstoppable. I encourage you to be
faithful right where you are, wherever you are"*[66]

— Christine Caine

Faithfulness is living the Christian life, faithfulness is being fully devoted and surrendered to the living God, and faithfulness is the embodied act of living out the gospel.

Salt and Light

In Matthew chapters five through seven, Jesus paints a picture of how He expects us to live a life of faithfulness. The backdrop of this scene is worth noting. Jesus sees enormous crowds of people following Him; some Bible translations say there are multitudes. Jesus climbs up on a mountainside and delivers what would be the famous Sermon on the Mount. In this sermon, Jesus articulates His expectations of how we should live in this world. Notice that this is not a private teaching to His disciples or an admonishment to the Pharisees and

Sadducees; instead, He gives these instructions to the crowds of ordinary people. He provides these instructions to the carpenters, the tax collectors, the doctors, the farmers, the shepherds, the merchants, and the fishermen. Translate those jobs to 2024. He gives these instructions to the computer science engineer, the teacher, the nurse, the individual contributor, the financial consultant, the leader, the Lyft driver, and the sales professional. He is speaking to the ordinary human being; He is speaking to you and me.

In Matthew 5:13–16 Jesus says:

> *You are the salt of the earth. But if the salt loses its saltiness, how can it be made salty again? It is no longer good for anything, except to be thrown out and trampled underfoot. You are the light of the world. A town built on a hill cannot be hidden. Neither do people light a lamp and put it under a bowl. Instead they put it on its stand, and it gives light to everyone in the house. In the same way, let your light shine before others, that they may see your good deeds and glorify your Father in heaven.*

Skye Jethani emphasizes the people Jesus instructs to be Salt and Light. He says:

> *His listeners were no one special. Still, Jesus said to these average, ordinary people, "You are the salt of the earth.... You are the light of the world." It's the scope of the statement that ought to surprise us. He didn't call them the salt or light of Galilee, but the world.*

Forget the Caesars, and Herods, and Platos. The world doesn't need more YouTube stars or social media celebrities. Jesus affirms the world-shaping value of ordinary people who follow the ways of an extraordinary God.

It isn't that He expected each person to change the world through remarkable accomplishments. Rather, Jesus expected His undistinguished followers to be the source of the world's most essential ingredients. Pliny, who lived in the first century, commented that there is nothing more useful in the world than "salt and sunshine." Likewise, in a dark, deteriorating world, there is nothing more wonderful than simple people living as Jesus taught.

To be the salt and light of the world does not require a person to do extraordinary acts or amass spectacular influence. The world does not need more ambitious Christians. Rather, salt and light are the outcomes of ordinary lives lived in rich communion with God. Our world desperately needs more of those.[67]

I love how he puts this. "Salt and light are the outcomes of ordinary lives lived in rich communion with God." Demonstrating the fruit of faithfulness is living in rich communion with God. This is living a life devoted to King Jesus and living out the gospel. The emphasis is not on doing an extraordinarily good deed. Nor is it a couple of remarkable acts. It is not in lavish or showy ways. Instead, it is in following Jesus step by step, moment by moment, throughout the course of your life. When you do this, you live a life that looks like Jesus.

Following Jesus produces the fruit and the character of Jesus in our lives. This is essential for us as we live out the Great Commission in our workplace.

Derek Vreeland notes:

> *We can be the soul—the salt and light, if you will—in our local communities by living as the people of love and mercy. In the face of mistrust, we offer faith. In the face of despair, we offer hope. In the face of hate, we offer love. If we are willing to look remarkably different than the world as we love one another, then we have a chance, not to change the world, but to bear witness to the world of the alternative and life-giving way of Jesus.[68]*

My Story

It was 2014, and things were going well with my career. I had worked my way up to senior director and had approximately 350 people on my team. My team, dispersed across the West Coast, was doing excellent work delivering IT services for the customers in our healthcare system. Late in the year, our overall IT team faced the challenge of saving money. As a result, my leader scheduled an in-person meeting with his direct reports. We all flew to Phoenix, and in the meeting, he announced he intended to restructure his department completely. The move he proposed was devastating to me. If implemented, it would have resulted in me losing direct responsibility for the vast majority of my team, as my department would shift down to about five people.

We spent the afternoon working together to devise a way to implement his desired changes. I was sick to my stomach. My people wouldn't want this. It was a mistake to decentralize, but I couldn't get my point across without looking defensive. I discerned that I needed to listen and be slow to speak. I just wanted to go home. In the end, I left there, and the decision was to leave me with a five-person governance team and decentralize everyone else. I was beside myself and quite disappointed. I sat on the plane in shock during the flight home.

Later that night, when I got home, I went to my backyard and called my best friend. She was an executive in the Information Technology department, and when I explained to her what happened, she was as stunned as I was by the trajectory of the meeting. My department had an excellent reputation; it didn't seem wise to break up this team, and neither of us could figure out the benefit of doing that. I cried; she offered advice, and when we hung up an hour later, I felt less alone, but it wasn't resolved. I didn't feel like the changes we were about to make were the right thing to do, but deep down, I was most upset that I had let Jesus down.

You see, for a long time, I couldn't believe I was supposed to be a leader. I hadn't gotten my college degree. I had worked my way up. I felt solely unqualified to lead this 300+ person team, but I knew it was my calling to do it and also I loved it. On the concrete in the backyard, I knelt down and wept. I sought forgiveness for neglecting to share the gospel with these people, despite having the opportunity for years. Despite being their leader, well respected, and loved by my people, I had failed to share anything about Jesus with them. I don't typically make deals with God, but I made a deal with God that day. If God would help me figure out how to keep the team, I promised I would not let another day go by without them knowing that I was a Christian and loved Jesus. I would make sure that my people heard the gospel.

I began praying for wisdom every single day. The following week, I walked into my leader's office, intending to get him to postpone the change until after the holidays. Before walking in, I prayed, "God, give me the right words. God, give me wisdom and strength, ease any emotions and fears that I have. These are your people, not mine, but please help me figure out how to get more time with them." I walked in, met with my boss, and told him that December was a terrible month to make these organizational changes and that we needed to push it out. He agreed, and we settled on announcing the changes in January. Every single time I met with him, I prayed for the right words, wisdom, and strength. I was able to delay again and again while Laura supported me along the way.

One day, our Chief Information Officer, Deanna Wise, called me. We talked about my perspective and I told her I thought this was a bad idea. I outlined why and she listened and asked questions along the way. About a week later, I got a call from my leader, who told me that Deanna wanted nothing touched in my organization. Thanks be to God!

That year, I would send over fifty people to a Christ-centered leadership conference. I heard from many that their lives had changed because of what they heard while attending. Some of my team members looked at Christianity differently than before. And I know that the conference transformed lives.

In the coming years, I would open conference attendance to additional organization members, and many people heard the Good News. One leader on my team, Thaddeus, suggested that we start openly praying before in-person meals. From then on, Thaddeus would direct our entire team to hold hands and lead us in prayer before meals. Our leadership team was openly giving thanks to God.

What I didn't know then was that my faith transformation would continue and that, over the next year, I would fall in love with Jesus in a new way. In a way that made more sense to me than anything I had heard or experienced up to this point. The teaching that changed my life was an in-depth study of the Sermon on the Mount. It was called Kingdom Culture and was taught by my pastor, Reverend Tara Beth Leach.

She called the Sermon on the Mount difficult; she said it could make us uncomfortable, and we might squirm. As Christians, she informed us we frequently simplify things to make them more bearable. This made sense because I had never heard it the way I was being taught now. It was indeed difficult and uncomfortable to hear. Leach says:

> *There's something particularly special about Jesus'*
> *Sermon on the Mount. The Sermon on the Mount is*
> *for those who are truly all in for the Christian life.*
> *What I mean by that is, we can't read the Sermon on*
> *the Mount and be somewhat in. We simply can't tone*
> *it down or soften it. Jesus asks for all of us. He asks for*
> *our obedience, our minds, our hearts, our emotions,*

our character, our decisions, our finances, our talents,
and our relationships – all with him at the center, as
the guide, and as the authority.[69]

Over the course of the next seven years, my faith would be challenged in ways I never expected, and it would grow exponentially. I read and studied the Bible. I asked questions and learned I had more questions than answers, but more faith than I had ever known.

In 2014, I knew God wanted more from me in this place. My role and influence would expand for the next nine years, and I remained faithful to God, the mission, and my teams. Through a merger in 2019, I became a Vice President and my team more than doubled in size. My travel increased, work complexities became significant, and in healthcare information technology, we survived the very long season of COVID, but nothing prepared me for what 2023 would bring.

A restructuring was coming, and as a result my leadership team and I were going to be laid off. As a senior leader known for valuing the ministry, they included me in the process, but the entire situation devastated me. Many of my team members had worked with me for over twenty years. We, indeed, were like family. Some people say that having a work family is toxic language, but I always say that just means they don't know how to do it right. We knew how to do it and this change was personal and hurtful. I could have stayed with the organization, and my leader encouraged me to. It was the safe decision; it was the financially sound decision. I was praying and discerning what I should do when one day on the phone with my leader, the Spirit of God washed over me, and I knew that my work was finished. While filled with grief, I was at complete peace that God was leading me in a new yet uncertain direction. It truly was the peace that passes all understanding that is spoken about in Philippians 4:7.

I was a connected leader to the frontline employees. As we got closer to when the restructuring was to be announced, I thought about where I should be the morning of the announcement. I didn't want to be at home, looking through a monitor. I wanted to be with my team, but they were scattered across the United States. Recognizing that my Arizona team would be one of the most emotionally affected, I made my way to Phoenix. We scheduled a team meeting, and I was by their side when they received the news. The room was full of pain, tears, and hugs. Each team meeting that followed over Zoom was full of weeping. At one point, our HR business partner said, "Few people usually care when senior leaders are let go. I have never seen anything like this." I had expected the team to be angry, but anger wasn't the emotion we saw; it was profound shock and grief.

During those first two days of the announcement, I felt like I was attending my own funeral. The grief and sadness were not just palpable; grown men were openly weeping. The gratitude from the team towards their leadership was unmeasurable. At meetings, one by one, people gave examples of specific times I had shown how much I loved them or what I did for them and the team. One call went on for almost two hours as stories were shared from around the country. Many of them were similar, and while each made me openly weep, some also made me laugh through my tears.

When Christian Galindo heard the news, I wasn't expecting him to have much of a sad reaction. Through the restructuring, he was getting a better job opportunity, and I was happy for him, but when he heard that his leader and I were leaving the company, his lip quivered, and his head fell to the desk. Like so many others, he sat there in a puddle of tears; when he looked back up at his Zoom camera, he said, "My life was changed seven years ago because Kim stopped me in a hallway and talked to me." I immediately recalled the moment. It was in 2016. We were activating a new electronic health record in Merced, California. Christian was a contractor who was doing a particularly great job. I stopped him, asked him if he was Christian, and told him, "I have heard good things about you." I then spent ten minutes talking to him about his future career. The next day, the same story repeated itself many times. Each time, I remembered the interaction. I wasn't doing anything revolutionary. I was present, listening, guiding, and showing people they mattered and that I was "*for* them."

I'll never forget what one particular person said, my younger brother, Andrew. Since 2014, Andrew had worked on my team under one of my leaders. He was exceptional at his job and, as a result, had worked his way up to team leader. When he spoke up in front of approximately 350 people, he said, "Hi everybody! If you don't know me, I'm Andrew, Kim's brother." Through tears, he went on, "Kim confided in me a while ago that this was going to happen, and I want you all to know that the only thing Kim has talked about leading up to this is how you will be affected. Every action she has taken was for us. She has shown no concern for herself. She loves all of us so much, and I just want her to know that I'm so proud of her, and I'm so proud to be her brother."

As these team members told stories, I became profoundly grateful for the opportunity my leaders and I had as we exited the organization. Most people subject to a layoff do not receive that type of exit. Thank you, Leah Miller.

My team and I put together a robust plan to transition out of the organization as faithfully as we had led. We provided training to new leaders; we made ourselves available for career development conversations, and while we all collectively grieved, we didn't throw in the towel. As we neared our final days, we assisted in every way we could. Just like I knew I had unfinished work nine years ago, this time, I knew I had completed my work here. Faithfulness kept us honoring our people and setting them up for success through our last days. Faithfulness kept us embodying the love of God and showing the love of God even as we have moved on to unemployment and new jobs. I can't help but think of 2 Timothy 4:7: "You have fought the good fight, you have finished the race, you have kept the faith." Just as God gave me peace that it was time to leave, I also have peace that I am being called to something different. There were moments when I had anxiety over not being employed, but I knew God was faithful and would work with me to write the next chapter.

That summer, I took time off to reexamine my priorities and refresh my soul. I rested, and we went on a family vacation to Hawaii. I tried new things, putting my hands to work for the first time, and I renovated my RV. My colleague and friend Faith (a woman with many skills) flew in and helped. My husband pitched in on the electrical and answered so many questions. I became a frequent flier at Home Depot. It was a fun, hard, and a learning experience. The RV now feels like a sacred space. I had decided months earlier that I would take a trip with my parents to the north rim of the Grand Canyon. This was a bucket list item for my mom, and my plan was to work on finishing *The Sacred Cubicle* and, when I returned, begin looking for work.

I sat in a rocking chair overlooking the Grand Canyon. The sky was bright blue with a few clouds in the distance. The canyon was massive and our front porch sat right on its rim. Across from me I could see the red, orange, yellow, and brown canyon walls with forest green shrubbery scattered around. Other than the sounds of birds chirping, all was quiet. I began editing the chapter on goodness. As I sat there, I began thinking about Ascension Health's Abide values and decided that I would include them in this chapter. I had friends and colleagues who worked at Ascension and one had shared about how deeply they embrace their values. I researched them, then wrote about what I had learned, finishing the goodness chapter.

We left the Grand Canyon the next morning. When we got back into cell service, my phone beeped, showing I had a voicemail. My mouth fell open when I played it. Someone at Ascension Health had called and asked if I, along with my team members, were available to come work at a couple of their hospitals. I was dumbfounded. Only God, and the work done through His people. Less than a week later, the team and I began working, supporting the ministry of Ascension Health. Thanks be to God.

Jesus' Call for Faithfulness

Jesus asks us to follow Him faithfully. He asks us to grow in Christlikeness. I mentioned early on how the Sermon on the Mount was transformative for me. This is because it is packed with life's guidance and instruction. There is so much richness, from the Beatitudes to Salt and Light to the Lord's Prayer. Hundreds of books, commentaries, and Bible studies have been written on Jesus' words in this passage. Jesus is calling His followers to a level of righteousness that is even higher than before. He is calling His followers to lean into the future Kingdom of God. I am going to unpack a few items from the sermon that directly relate to how we conduct a life of faithfulness in our workplaces.

Jesus references Old Testament scripture and then raises the ask of the people. He starts with murder, saying, "You have heard that it was said to the people long ago, 'You shall not murder, and anyone who murders will be subject to judgment.' But I tell you that anyone who is angry with a brother or sister will be subject to judgment." He instructs those with a grievance with someone else to go to that person and quickly resolve it. This instruction is critical for our witness in this world. We encounter these situations daily.

Most people reading this can recall a time when someone angered them, and rather than going to that person to reconcile, they allowed it to fester. They may have told someone else about it. They may have become bitter. Reconciliation isn't always easy. In fact, it's usually challenging. Going to the person to address the issue may cause discomfort and anxiety, but Jesus expects us to do the difficult thing. He emboldens us to have courage and not let fear stop us from doing what we

know is right. I can't pretend that I am great at this. I am con-
flict-avoidant, and it seems so much easier to shy away from
the problem, but that is not what we are supposed to do.

Once I worked with an incredibly abrasive woman. During
conference calls, it was not uncommon to receive text emojis of
eye rolls or comments about how irritating she was. At times,
I have initiated that type of communication. It's not a good
witness, nor is it Christ-like. It is not salt and light. I recall one
Zoom call when I received a text from a colleague that said,
"Kim, your face looks like it's had enough." These behaviors
or expressions matter when we are representing God in our
workplace.

Matthew 5 verses 43–48 says:

> *You have heard that it was said, 'Love your neighbor
> and hate your enemy.' But I tell you, love your enemies
> and pray for those who persecute you, that you may be
> children of your Father in heaven. He causes his sun
> to rise on the evil and the good, and sends rain on the
> righteous and the unrighteous. If you love those who
> love you, what reward will you get? Are not even the
> tax collectors doing that? And if you greet only your
> own people, what are you doing more than others? Do
> not even pagans do that? Be perfect, therefore, as your
> heavenly Father is perfect.*

It's so easy to love the people you like at work. The ones
with the same work ethic as you, those you see eye to eye with
on the strategic vision, the person who is consistently delivering

for you right when you need them. It's so much harder to love those who make work difficult.

My friend had a big meeting on the morning of her birthday. She was pitching a service to a new customer, and it was one of her first in-person customer meetings post-COVID. There had been extensive preparation for this meeting. She was excited to share the excellent work her team had accomplished. In her mind, her customer would be wowed by the content. Halfway through the presentation, the customer became upset and began to yell at her. He was rude and unprofessional, which was the last thing she and the others in the room expected. Taken off guard and dejected, she sat in her car afterward, crying from frustration. She shouldn't have been treated that way, and of all days, her fiftieth birthday! I imagine it would be hard for her to love this customer. And yet, that's what Jesus tells us to do: love our enemies.

My friend is a Christian; let's look at this scenario keeping in mind the last two sections of Scripture, and let's learn from how she responded to the situation.

What she did:

- She privately grieved the situation—demonstrating the fruit of peace.
- She prayed—demonstrating the fruit of goodness.
- She called on another Christian as a trusted advisor to talk through the situation—demonstrating the fruit of faithfulness.
- She called her customer and told him she was working on addressing his

concerns—demonstrating the fruit of kindness and love.

- She moved forward with grace, hoping and praying for resolution—demonstrating the fruit of patience.

What she didn't do:

- Yell back at him—demonstrating the fruit of gentleness
- Ignore the issue—demonstrating the fruit of goodness
- Call colleagues to complain about him—demonstrating the fruit of self-control

As we can see from this simple example, the fruit of the Spirit can be shown not just in our actions, but even in our inaction.

Jesus provided several examples, reminding His followers not to boast about their Christian practices. In his warning, he advised us against being hypocrites or showy. Giving to the needy is something he instructs us to do, but without publicly announcing it. He shows us how to pray and reminds us not to flaunt our prayers. He gives us the Lord's prayer and says, "And when you pray, do not be like the hypocrites, for they love to pray standing in the synagogues and on the street corners to be seen by others." Each of us should take these reminders and commands from Jesus seriously. I know when I read them, I am struck by how my actions, even this book, could be read by some as hypocritical. This book has been written by a flawed Christian who is taking steps to walk moment by moment in the power of the Spirit of the Living God. Every day, I stumble. Every day, I pray that God's Spirit continues to transform me into Christlikeness.

This Christian life embodies love, joy, peace, patience, kindness, goodness, gentleness, faithfulness, and self-control. It's consistently leaning into the Spirit of the living God. We won't always get it right. We won't always reflect the perfect image of Jesus, but if we are faithfully walking with the Spirit, others will notice us bearing witness to our perfect God.

Tips and Biblical Encouragement

How can we practice faithfulness in our workplace?

1. Remember your why. As Christians, God and God's mission are the why behind our faithfulness. Our motivation is not for success, financial security, or pride, but because we love the Lord our God.

    A faithful person will be richly blessed, but one eager to get rich will not go unpunished.

    — Proverbs 28:20

2. Faithfulness is not obsessing about our worries but giving them to God instead.

    Cast all your anxiety on him because he cares for you.

    — 1 Peter 5:7

3.   Ensure you are living a life that is constantly being transformed. Practice spiritual formation, pray, read the Bible, and commune with God.

And we all, who with unveiled faces contemplate the Lord's glory, are being transformed into his image with ever-increasing glory, which comes from the Lord, who is the Spirit.

— 2 Corinthians 3:18

4.   Our lives are a testament to our faithfulness. People will take note if we embody the fruit of the Spirit.

It gave me great joy when some believers came and testified about your faithfulness to the truth, telling how you continue to walk in it.

— 3 John 1:5

5.   Remember the Shema, the greatest commandment, and live it out.

"Hear, O Israel: The Lord our God, the Lord is one. Love the Lord your God with all your heart and with all your soul and with all your strength."

— Deuteronomy 6:4–5

6.   Remember that Jesus amended the Shema in the New Testament. Take heart of what He calls the second

greatest commandment and live according to His words:

"And the second is like it: 'Love your neighbor as yourself.'"

— Matthew 22:39

Reflective Questions

1. How can I actively embody the qualities of salt and light in my everyday interactions and decisions, ensuring that my actions glorify God and make a positive impact on those around me?

2. How does my commitment to faithfulness in my current role reflect my understanding of God's faithfulness to me?

3. In what practical ways can I offer faith, hope, and love in my community, especially when faced with mistrust, despair, or hate?

4. How can I ensure that, like Paul, I am fighting the good fight, finishing the race, and keeping the faith in my current circumstances? What does faithfulness look like in my current season of life?

5. How can I recognize and embrace the potential for ordinary, everyday actions to shape the world positively, rather than seeking extraordinary achievements?

6. What lessons can I draw from my experiences to enhance my walk with God and my witness to others?

CHAPTER 9

Love

Agape is disinterested love… Agape does not begin by discriminating between worthy and unworthy people, or any qualities people possess. It begins by loving others for their sakes… Therefore, agape makes no distinction between friend and enemy; it is directed toward both.[70]

— Martin Luther King Jr.

Love at work. At first blush, that sounds complicated, problematic, and a human resources nightmare. When we delve into the Bible's teachings on love, we can unravel its application in the workplace, turning it from being seen as inappropriate to being viewed as a necessary aspect for a productive and flourishing work setting.

For years, I have said, "Leaders are called to love their people." This has proved controversial because it contradicts what most leaders in the corporate world are taught. Leaders are to inspire, provide direction, collaborate, and give a strategic vision. I have never been in a leadership class that told me leaders were to love. It seems weird, it might be uncomfortable, and it may sound counterintuitive to every leadership training you have attended. As contrarian as it might be, I have come to the unshakable belief that love and developing a character of love in our lives and our leadership is the bedrock from which we grow.

While still rare, the tides are starting to change on the concept of love in the workplace. I used to feel alone in this idea, but best-selling author Marcus Buckingham recently launched a new book, and the title may surprise; it's called *Love + Work*. He also started a new website in partnership with *Harvard Business Review*; you can find it at "loveandwork.org." Buckingham talks about love at work from a different angle— he talks about how it's important for us to love our work. He says:

> *There's a lot of people writing these days about how you shouldn't expect your job to love you back. They say your work is not your family; your work is trans-actional. Stop expecting of it something that it can't deliver. Yet when you study people who are really, really good at what they do—and I don't think this will be a surprise to anyone—they find love in what they do. The most successful people do what they love. That seems like a nice aphorism, but there's no data to support it. There is a lot of data that the most success-ful people find the love in what they do. You might be confronting someone or presenting or performing a particular aspect of an operation or caring for a student. Whatever it is, if it's one of the things that you love, you'll have a chemical cocktail present in your brain: dopamine, oxytocin, norepinephrine, and anandamide.*

We know what that does to your brain. We know it deregulates the egoic part of your neocortex, which is focused on outcomes and goal achievement. It deregulates that, and your mind gets opened to more information and inputs, and it gets more comfortable with those inputs, so you measurably perform cognitive tasks better. Your memory's better; you're better at pointing out other people's emotions and naming them accurately, so you're more empathetic; and you're more creative.

When you're in love with another human, it makes you feel safe, it makes you feel inquisitive, and it makes you feel uplifted. It's the same cocktail when you're doing something that you love. If companies want creativity, if they want innovation, if they want resilience, and if they want engagement, they have to engage with the word love. [71]

Ekua Hagan published an article in *Psychology Today* entitled "What's Love Got to Do with Work." In the article, she says:

For some odd reason, we are uncomfortable with the word love at work. Maybe it's because we compartmentalize our lives and would prefer to leave that squishy love stuff to our personal relationships and home life. But I think it's a lot more complicated than that. At a time when business and society require us to be more authentic and connected, we find ourselves running away from intimacy and expressions of love.

This is not good for people, and it's definitely not good for business.

Love is arguably one of the most powerful human emotions. Love motivates and inspires us. It helps us rise above our personal needs and build organizations with a higher purpose. When you bring love into the workplace, you create positive and nourishing relationships.[72]

Biblical Love in the Workplace

Let's spend some time dissecting biblical love, and then we'll revisit my statement, "Leaders are called to love their people." *The Sacred Cubicle* was written for the ordinary worker, so I'm going to change that up a bit. "Christians are called to love their coworkers."

Even if you aren't a regular Bible reader, it's possible you have heard of 1 Corinthians 13. Written by the apostle Paul, you may have heard this passage read at weddings or referenced occasionally. The love chapter says this:

Love is patient, love is kind. It does not envy, it does not boast, it is not proud. It does not dishonor others; it is not self-seeking, it is not easily angered, it keeps no record of wrongs. Love does not delight in evil but rejoices with the truth. It always protects, always trusts, always hopes, always perseveres. Love never fails.

You will notice there are a couple of other fruits mentioned in the Bible's description of love. This shows an interdependent relationship between all of these characteristics of the Spirit. One who is walking in the Spirit will exhibit a character of love, and from that character, patience, kindness, and goodness. As goes the root, so goes the branches.

As I was preparing to write about love, I pondered these attributes of love. Other than "love keeping no records of wrongs," which we will unpack in a few pages, nothing here seems to contradict being a great leader, coworker, or employee.

Let's examine these attributes of love. We will spend more time on those we haven't reviewed in earlier chapters.

Love is patient: Think back to the chapter on patience. Are you practicing the discipline of patience in your work? Would those you work with say you are a patient person?

Love is kind: We have read about kindness extensively in *The Sacred Cubicle*. Do you exude kindness in your work?

Love does not envy: Do you find yourself jealous in the workplace? This trait is considered one of the deadly sins. I sometimes find myself envious of others' skills. My two closest friends are excellent speakers. They inspire me with their ability to think quickly and communicate clearly. I could listen to either of them speak for hours. I often wish I had the verbal communication skills they possess. Are you envious of others' skills or positions at work?

Love does not boast: Do you boast or show off? I sometimes wonder if my social media posts come across as boastful. For example, I love the national parks, and when I am on vacation, I often share videos of our epic views. I don't do this to be boastful but to share the beauty with my coworkers, friends, and families. At times, I have wondered, how does this come across? As social media has evolved, I have worked to use more discretion. In what ways could you be seen as boastful?

Love isn't proud: Pride is another one of the deadly sins. I often have to examine my heart for pride. What is healthy pride versus unhealthy pride, particularly in the workplace? I am unabashedly proud of my team's work throughout the last three years. Being information technology professionals in healthcare during a pandemic was demanding and challenging. I am proud of each of them for the times they stepped into a COVID patient's room so that they could be treated, for the times they helped connect a dying person with their family outside the hospital, for the effort they put in to build triage tents, for the times they set up vaccine clinics. Let's not forget every single day when they went to work, not knowing whether they would bring COVID-19 into their homes. I don't think this is the pride Paul is talking about.

Paul is talking about the pride of self. People who think they are better than others are prideful. This deadly sin resulted in Lucifer, aka Satan, being cast out of the Kingdom. In Isaiah 14, Lucifer declares himself to be equal to God. His pride resulted in him being removed from heaven and separated from God. Examine your heart. What selfish pride do you recognize?

Love does not dishonor: Are you respectful to others? One way I have fallen into dishonoring others is by not giving my full attention. Was I distracted by competing priorities? Was I talking over someone else in a meeting? Did I belittle an idea? Did I bow to hierarchy or treat all with the same level of respect?

Love is not self-seeking: It is always you before me. It is about what is in the best interest of the individual or the team, not what is in my best interest. Love means doing things for others that are of no benefit to yourself.

I have traveled a lot for work and I enjoy it. I get to spend time with our people in the hospitals, the people close to the customers, the people I love. Love sometimes means doing inconvenient or personally disruptive things for the people we work alongside. Remember, leaders are called to love their people, and this is one thing I am decent at. It was December 2009, and I was seven months pregnant, and I was over being pregnant and sick of traveling. An employee of mine was struggling, and I told his leader he needed some development. This employee took constructive criticism very personally, and I knew I would need to help deliver the news. I didn't want to go, but I arranged to fly out for this conversation because I knew my effort was necessary for his growth.

Love is not easily angered: We discussed the impact angry people can have during the chapter on Peace. Anger in this workplace is disruptive and leads to a toxic culture. If the person is a leader, it usually results in a culture of fear and an environment void of psychological safety. If the person is an individual contributor, it is often someone that people try to avoid or workaround. Ultimately, someone who gets angry easily rarely shows love towards others they interact with.

Love keeps no record of wrongs: This is challenging in the workplace. At work, we need people to perform at their jobs and at the organization's standards. As a leader, there are certain wrongs that I keep track of. I believe this is about how we treat wrongs in the workplace. Do we offer grace? Are we in the habit of nitpicking? Do we throw past mistakes in people's faces? Do we believe that generally, people are doing the best they can? This isn't asking us to look the other way, but it's asking us to be generous in addressing issues. We need to help people perform their best and avoid kicking them when they are down.

Love does not delight in evil but rejoices in the truth: When you see ethical problems and inappropriate behavior, do something. I once knew a leader who instructed all the leaders reporting to them not to report ethics violations to the company. As an employee of your company, it is imperative that you report ethical violations. If your company has an ethics hotline, use it! These lines are available to ensure the people in your organization are operating with integrity and following company guidelines and applicable laws. In this case, many leaders called the hotline. When you see evil, confront it.

Love always protects: During the early days of the COVID-19 pandemic, my team members were the only IT employees working at the hospitals. I ran into a situation where teams from another company were refusing to come in to do their work. We all were scared, yet my employees were coming in every day to ensure that our patients and caregivers had the tools they needed to work safely. It was hard being an essential worker in 2020. On an hourly basis, I navigated complexities regarding protective gear, COVID-19 protocols, illnesses, and team members going well beyond their jobs to ensure we could care for our patients. My actions were always about protecting my employees from illness, burnout, or stress. I wish I could say that none of my employees ever got sick or suffered from burnout, but I can't. Despite my efforts, most suffered burnout, and many were ill, but I know they know I did my best to protect them during a tumultuous time. Are you looking out for others?

Love always trusts: I trust relatively freely, sometimes too freely. Ronald Reagan used to say, "Trust, but verify." When I first heard that phrase, I didn't like it. Is that really trust? As I have considered it for many years, I have realized that verification is essential for certain things. If the stakes are high, trust walks hand in hand with protection. Trusting freely has come back to bite me, my leaders, my peers, and the people who work for me. Now, when the stakes are high, I verify. This ensures that the team member responsible is protected; maybe they didn't realize their assignment was a big deal. Perhaps they didn't know it needed to be completed in a certain way. Verification protects them.

Love always hopes: One year, I received a gift from an employee, Carlos. It was a framed inspirational poster that said, "The light of optimism." He said that was me. I am a dreamer, I am hopeful, and I am generally optimistic. At one point in my career, many employees were leaving the organization because, admittedly, things were deteriorating and seemingly always getting worse. I was routinely asked why I was still there, and my response was generally that I felt like things would get better. I knew God still wanted me there. I hoped things would get better, and I prayed things would get better. Love always hopes. While hope may not be a strategy, are you hoping for the best outcomes in your work? Are you catastrophizing problems or hoping for the success of others? Are you hopefully pitching in to help your coworkers?

Love always preserves: Love lasts. It's not fake. It's not fleeting. During a tough financial season, I had to reduce our workforce. One particular employee was especially hard for me. I scheduled a meeting with him and flew into his town to be there in person. He had a pretty good idea of what it was, and he didn't show up to meet, so we ended up having the conversation over the phone. He was angry, and I was fairly sure he wouldn't speak to me again. A few months later, though, I heard from him; he wanted me to review his resume and help him find a job. We began to talk somewhat regularly. I helped him with his resume, coached him through his interview process, and put in a good word for him with someone I knew at his prospective employer. I prayed for him and his family, and when he nailed the job, I celebrated with him. It's been years, and we still communicate. Love lasts.

Love never fails: Have you noticed that Paul's descriptions of love use the words always and never? Those are hard words. While Jesus tells us to be perfect in Matthew 5, which is what we strive for, we know that none of us are perfect. There was only one perfect human. As I read, love never fails, I think I have failed the people who work for me a thousand times. Never intentionally, but sometimes things didn't turn out as I thought. I think of the time I told Jeff that it was a little project I needed him to coordinate. Turns out, that project wasn't so little. It ended up sucking up six months of his life. I think about Mike, Eric, Joe, and Jacob when they got much more than they bargained for when I sent them to Tennessee on an assignment.

As people, we aren't perfect. We will fail sometimes, but it is in those moments of failure that our character emerges.

It's in reconciliation, and it's in asking for forgiveness. It's in saying you are sorry, meaning it, and adjusting your approach. When we are ruggedly committed to each other, failures are forgiven, and ultimately, the circle of love you created does not fail.

The Love Filter

As a regular act of self-reflection, I run myself through what I call the love filter. It is always illuminating as I quickly see where I have struggled to love and where I have been at my best. Self-examination and reflection through the love filter require one to look at their behaviors and ask themselves if they are reflecting the love of God through their actions or if they are reflecting the broken world. As Christ-centered people, we should desire to represent God's perfect love to the people around us so those we encounter will be drawn into curiosity about the Christian life and, ultimately, the beauty of God. People who are rooted in love make us feel seen and cared for. They create a sense of belonging, and so, as a follower of Jesus, we must show His love to those we encounter in the workplace.

First Corinthians 13:4–8 is the basis of the love filter.

Practicing the Love Filter

Begin the session in prayer. Pray for self-awareness. Ask God to give you an accurate view of your heart and how you show love in the workplace. Does your heart match your actions? My prayer often looks something like this:

God help open my eyes and see my behavior clearly.

Remove my defenses and blind spots.
Guide me through this process and remind me that
where I fall short, you can help me overcome. Make it
clear to me when I need to reconcile a situation.
Thank you for loving me just the way that I am.

Read Through 1 Corinthians 13.

Begin examining verses 4–8.

Review your last week and take notes as you go. Here is an example:

- **Love is patient:** I wanted our planning document completed by Tuesday, but when the team said they needed more time, we renegotiated the due date so it worked for everyone.
- **Love is kind:** I sent thank-you notes and acknowledged Brandon and his team's extra effort.
- **Love does not envy:** N/A
- **Love does not boast:** N/A
- **Love isn't proud:** Working with new people over the last week, I intentionally took a posture of curiosity and humility.
- **Love does not dishonor:** I spoke behind someone's back yesterday.
- **Love is not self-seeking:** I chose a testing date that was better for the rest of the team, even though it wasn't a convenient day for me.
- **Love is not easily angered:** I can't recall a time when I was angry this week.

- **Love keeps no record of wrongs:** N/A
- **Love does not delight in evil but rejoices in the truth:** N/A
- **Love always protects:** I protected Thaddeus's family time by ensuring he left the office on time.
- **Love always trusts:** I trusted the team could get through the details of a problem without my intervention. I verified by having the team report our progress.
- **Love always hopes:** Showed hope for turning a red status item to yellow by next week. I put a plan in place to reach the goal but ensured the team knew I had complete confidence in them, and I was hoping for success.
- **Love always preserves:** Last night, I had dinner with someone who worked for me in the past, and I have lunch scheduled with another former employee later this week. I am not their leader anymore, but I still invest in them. I still love them and am still *for* them. The feeling is mutual.
- **Love never fails:** I kept all my commitments this week.

When you have finished your self-examination, if you are comfortable, share your review with a trusted coworker or friend and see what they think. Don't ask someone to validate your perspective, but tell them what you are doing and ask them for their perspective.

Determine any actions you should take to reconcile or do better in the future.

Wrap the session in prayer. Thank God for giving you time to self-reflect and baseline how you show love to others at work.

The Greatest Commandment

We were instructed to love long before Paul wrote the chapter on love. Way back in the Old Testament, in Deuteronomy, we find the first and arguably the most notable scripture for the Jewish people, the Shema. Deuteronomy 6:4–6, "Hear, O Israel: The Lord our God, the Lord is one. Love the Lord your God with all your heart and with all your soul and with all your strength. These commandments that I give you today are to be on your hearts." In the New Testament, Jesus draws from the Shema when the Pharisees ask Him what the greatest commandment is.

Matthew 22:37–39 says, "'Love the Lord your God with all your heart and with all your soul and with all your mind.' This is the first and greatest commandment. And the second is like it: 'Love your neighbor as yourself.'"

We adopted a liturgy at the dinner table. We recite this command every night before thanking God for our food. It reminds us that these are the greatest two commands from Jesus. Loving God leads to loving neighbors. When we love God with all of our heart, all of our soul, all of our mind, and all of our strength, it's impossible for us not to love our neighbors as well.

Love your neighbor as yourself. When I was a kid, I used to think this command meant that I needed to love the angry next-door neighbor to the north and the friendly Jewish couple to the south of our house, and that was it. The truth is, I found the lovely Jewish couple a lot easier to love than our cranky neighbor next door to the north. It wasn't until years later that I realized that when Jesus said neighbor, He basically meant everyone who comes into contact with me. That is a lot of love to spread around. Even harder, in the Sermon on the Mount, He instructed us to love our enemies.

Loving our enemies is difficult. Only through the power of the Spirit can we do this. I alone am not capable of loving my enemies. In the workplace, enemies often throw up roadblocks, are self-absorbed, and make things difficult for our customers and colleagues. It's not always easy to love these people, but that's precisely what we have been commanded to do.

Jesus gives us the commands in Matthew, and Paul gives us a beautiful depiction of what love is in 1 Corinthians. When we follow the commands, lean into the Spirit, and our life overflows with love, people will see it, take note of it, and become curious about your life.

Levi King wrote an article for *Inc. Magazine* on showing employees you love them. He notes, "Expressing love to your employees energizes, motivates and inspires them. It'll do the same thing for you."[73] He notes we should learn the stories of those we work with, and I couldn't agree more. Knowing people's stories demonstrates you care about who they are, not just what they produce as your teammates or employees.

I have worked with some of my team members for a very long time. Aaron Nance and I have worked together for over twenty years. We knew each other long before we had kids. Aaron and I entered the workforce early and hadn't finished our college degrees. Both of us regretted it, so in 2016, we returned to college together. As forty-somethings, we received our bachelor's degrees from Azusa Pacific University. We have gone through outsourcing, insourcing, mergers, and acquisitions together. Recently, during a 1:1 meeting, he was telling me about his father-in-law, who moved in with him and his wife so that they could care for him. We discussed our history, friendship, time at work, and how we are now approaching significant life events with our parents. We have done life together; we know the names of each other's kids. I know he prefers Dutch Bros to Starbucks and that his daughter is a champion swimmer. I know he is a foodie, and we have hunted down the best eats in the geographies we visit for work and play. Aaron knows I love him; Aaron knows that my love for him extends to his family.

Tips and Biblical Encouragement

While the love chapter tells us how to love, there is no more extraordinary love story than God sending His only Son, Jesus, to live, dwell, and begin restoration of the earth through His life, death, and resurrection. In the resurrection, Jesus overturns death, He overturns evil, and ultimately, He sits as King at the right hand of God. As you reflect on how you can show love in the workplace, I encourage you to run yourself through the love filter and use the following tips to cultivate love further.

In the NIV Bible, love is mentioned 538 times. As I wrap up this chapter on love, let's remember that in the end, three things remain: faith, hope, and love, and the greatest is love.

1. I find the most challenging time for me to love is when dealing with difficult people. My version of the workplace enemy is people that are difficult to get along with. Take two minutes before your meetings and look at the participant list. Is there anyone there that you don't want to interact with? If so, ask the Lord to give you love, kindness, and patience towards that person.

   But love your enemies, do good to them, and lend to them without expecting to get anything back. Then your reward will be great, and you will be children of the Most High, because he is kind to the ungrateful and wicked.

   — Luke 6:35

2. Be a listener. Listen to your leaders, peers, subordinates, and customers. There are many verses on listening, whether you are listening to learn or listening to help someone. Being present and paying attention to people when they are talking shows love and respect.

   The way of fools seems right to them, but the wise listen to advice.

   — Proverbs 12:15

3. Break bread with your teammates. Levi King noted in his article that if you are a leader, you should "wine and dine" your employees. He says, "There's something glorious about gathering with friends and colleagues to

enjoy good food and drink. Psychological walls come down, talk and laughter flow, and you leave the table closer in mind and Spirit than when you sat down." He's right, and Jesus was our example of this. He routinely conducted ministry around the table, and so should we.

While Jesus was having dinner at Levi's house, many tax collectors and sinners were eating with him and his disciples, for there were many who followed him. When the teachers of the law, who were Pharisees, saw him eating with the sinners and tax collectors, they asked his disciples: "Why does he eat with tax collectors and sinners?" On hearing this, Jesus said to them, "It is not the healthy who need a doctor, but the sick. I have not come to call the righteous, but sinners."

— Mark 2:15–17

4. Show grace. Because God loved us, God gave us the gift of grace, even though we didn't deserve it. God saved us through grace; if we are walking in the Spirit and trying to live like Jesus, we should always err on grace rather than condemnation.

Reflective Questions

1. In what ways do you show kindness to your colleagues, and how does this align with the instruction to "love your neighbor as yourself"?

2. Are there situations at work where you struggle with envy? How can you overcome these feelings and embody the biblical principle that "love does not envy" (1 Corinthians 13:4)?

3. Have there been times when you've unintentionally dishonored someone at work? How can you ensure that your actions and words honor others?

4. How do you prioritize the needs of others over your own in your professional life?

5. How do you maintain hope and optimism in challenging work situations? How does your approach reflect the biblical teaching that "love always hopes"?

Living the Great Commission

> *Then I heard the voice of the Lord saying, "Whom shall I send? And who will go for us?" And I said, "Here am I. Send me!"*
>
> — the Prophet Isaiah; Isaiah 6:8

Bearing Witness

The Sacred Cubicle contends that the first step to fulfilling our roles in the Great Commission is living a life that bears a resemblance to Jesus. A life that shows the fruit of the Holy Spirit in us. The characteristics of love, joy, peace, patience, kindness, goodness, gentleness, faithfulness, and self-control, abundantly flowing out of our life.

Walking a Spirit-filled life in an upside-down world isn't an easy thing to do. Being known as a Christian today can be daunting. It can cause people to make assumptions about you—and unfortunately, most times, the assumptions look nothing like Jesus. Sin, hypocrisy, and moral failures have run rampant in the church and tarnished the view of Christians. We see self-proclaiming Christians behave opposite to the God we are supposed to be reflecting. As image bearers, it is critical we restore our credibility. By leaning into the power of the Spirit, we can restore our image and become radiant witnesses.

Living a life of salt and light, loving our neighbors and our enemies, is the first part. Those around you will notice the difference in you, but if they don't know the why, then we are falling short.

Evangelism Rooted in Fear

Every year on New Year's Day, we have about a hundred people show up at our house for the Tournament of Roses Parade. We live on the parade route and open our home to friends, family, and the neighborhood. It's an exhausting but exhilarating tradition in our home. At the end of the parade there is always a group of people carrying signs that say things like "Repent, for the end of the world is near," or "Cursed are you," or "Choose Jesus or burn." These people carry loud microphones with speakers and are desperately urging people to turn from sin or die in fire. Most onlookers do not take their message seriously and view them as deranged. Some categorize all Christians by their actions. These likely well-intended people are trying to convert people to Christianity, but their message lacks wisdom and has the opposite effect. They use the Bible as a weapon to coerce non-believers. And they use one of the arguably strongest human emotions, fear, to do it. But 1 John 4:18 says, "There is no fear in love. But perfect love drives out fear, because fear has to do with punishment. The one who fears is not made perfect in love."

Weaponizing Scripture, often referred to as beating people over the head with the Bible, does not show the love of God. Have you ever been in a conversation where someone used the Bible as a weapon against you? It's not a great tactic if you are looking for an honest, loving, and kind conversation. I think Christians who do this are trying to be good evangelizers, but they are so consumed by their beliefs they lose sight of all else. Rather than engaging with a listening ear and seeking to understand the other, they spend their time formulating their response. What verse will they use in rebuttal? Most often, they are seeking only to convert to their way of thinking, but this method typically backfires. Here are some examples of weaponizing Scripture:

1. Using out-of-context verses to justify personal biases.
2. Employing scripture to condemn or judge others instead of leaving judgement to God.
3. Using Scripture to shame or guilt individuals into conversion.
4. Using the Bible to assert moral superiority over others.
5. Using Scripture to justify discrimination or exclusion of certain groups.

6. Employing biblical teachings as a tool for manipulation or emotional abuse in relationships.

The Good News

Romans 5:8 tell us: "But God demonstrates his own love for us in this: While we were still sinners, Christ died for us."

The Gospel is the gift of salvation. Through Jesus' life, death, and resurrection, evil is overturned! This means we have:

- forgiveness of sins
- an identity in Christ
- gifts of grace and mercy
- healing of sickness
- empowerment from the Holy Spirit
- freedom from guilt and shame
- reconciliation in our relationships
- victory over death
- hope for the future

And that is just the beginning. That is Good News and it needs to be shared! James Choung says:

> Good news is not meant to be held back. We're wired
> to tell someone about it. Whether it's a good book,
> an inspiring movie, a job promotion, a luxurious
> getaway, a catchy song, an exhilarating hike or a

*random encounter with an old friend, we really can't
wait to grab someone and load them up with the
details.*[74]

The message we share is one of Good News! It's one we
should want to shout from the rooftops in celebration! When
our team wins the Super Bowl, we celebrate; when our kids
win awards, we post it on our socials; when we return from
vacation, we can't wait to tell people the highlights. All of
these pale in comparison to the Good News we have to share.
We have Good News, and to fulfill the Great Commission, we
need to share it.

Evangelism in Action

Part of our assignment from God is to build community and
relationships in this world. For evangelism, nothing beats relationship building, but remember that if your only goal is conversion, you'll miss out on the beauty of authentic mutual connections. Building relationships with others is one of the most
critical functions of being a Christian. In her book, *Radiant
Church*, Pastor Tara Beth Leach wrote about me saying:

> *Kim is one of those people who makes everyone feel
> like they are the most important person in the room.
> Kim loves people, and people know that when they are
> around. Kim shows her love by helping other mammas
> with school pick up, or volunteering to help set up a
> party, or throwing a neighborhood pool party, or going
> out of her way to help a distressed co-worker. Kim is*

also an evangelist. There have been several occasions where she has shared her love for King Jesus with a neighbor, but it's never because she sees said neighbor as a project or means to an end. Evangelism, for Kim, comes out of sincere love and neighborliness.

But before she ever even shares the good news of Jesus, she embodies the gospel power in all that she does. Before words, she bears witness to the love, joy, peace, patience, kindness, goodness, gentleness, and generosity of the kingdom. The gospel, when reduced to a presentation, is severely malnourished. The gospel is something we bear witness to; it is something we embody, it is something we live. By the time Kim ever shares the good news, it has been seen.[75]

Her account in *Radiant Church* humbles me, and I pray I live up to her observations. I haven't always, and I know I have unintentionally hurt people. Some may disagree with how Tara Beth views me. I recognize these flaws, these sins, and a few names come to mind that deserve apologies from me.

The Great Commission

I love The Message translation for the Great Commission. It says:

Jesus, undeterred, went right ahead and gave His charge: "God authorized and commanded me to commission you: Go out and train everyone you meet, far and near, in this way of life, marking them by baptism

in the threefold name: Father, Son, and Holy Spirit.
Then instruct them in the practice of all I have com-
manded you. I'll be with you as you do this, day after
day after day, right up to the end of the age.

Jesus' words here literally choke me up. God has invited
us to participate in reconciling this world! In the business
world, we often say "we want a seat at the table," indicating
that we want to be invited into higher-level conversations and
meetings. Folks, there is no higher seat at the table than this.
We have been invited and commanded to be a part of God's
almighty plan to restore the earth! God could do this alone,
but instead, God counts on us to mediate his goodness to this
weary world.

Romans 10:13–15 says:

> *For, "Everyone who calls on the name of the Lord*
> *will be saved." How, then, can they call on the one*
> *they have not believed in? And how can they believe*
> *in the one of whom they have not heard? And how*
> *can they hear without someone preaching to them?*
> *And how can anyone preach unless they are sent? As*
> *it is written: "How beautiful are the feet of those who*
> *bring good news!"*

Sharing the Good News requires wisdom and listening
to the Spirit. Rich Villodas wrote, "The announcement of the
gospel is a practice that requires careful discernment, compassionate curiosity and a willingness to step beyond a transaction
of faith."[76] If we aren't wise, our words can backfire and turn

people away rather than towards the living God. Some of the ways that I evangelize the Word of God are:

- Build sincere and authentic relationships with others.
- Pray about and for those around you. Ask the Spirit for wisdom in how and when to share the Good News of your Savior with others.
- Be open about your faith at work. Place a Bible on your desk and read it. (Don't just use it as a prop.) When debriefing your weekend, mention the church you go to. Don't be ashamed of being a Christian.
- People will often respond to invitations. Invite people to special events at your church, like Christmas or Easter services. When my kids were baptized, I invited my neighbors.
- Use your social media in a way that honors God. Share your church livestream or events.
- Be open and listen to the Spirit's prompting.

I love how Pastor Rich sums up how ultimately sharing the story of the gospel is simply faith in action. He says:

> *Every person, at some point, will undergo a power-lessness that leads to despair. As we offer our presence, lovingly and patiently listening to others, we will find ourselves in a better space to non coercively offer words of hope, announcing that Christ is present and worthy of trust.*

*To announce the gospel in a deeply formed way
moves us beyond techniques and one-size-fits-all strategies. As Jesus perfectly modeled, we are called to open
ourselves to joining the journeys of others, building
relationship, discerning openness, and announcing
the news of God's loving presence and commitment
toward them. This is not cookie-cutter evangelism,
and we will find ourselves unsure of how to move
forward. But this is the nature of faith, isn't it?*[77]

The Albuquerque International Balloon Fiesta started in 1972 with thirteen balloons and it has grown steadily ever since. In 2023, almost a million people attended to watch approximately six hundred balloons take flight over the Chihuahuan desert. Another 700K watched the event live online.[78] This fiesta is a celebration. The vibe is exciting, and it contagiously spreads through the gathered crowd. Before the balloons ascend into the sky, careful preparation is undertaken to ensure safety and success, from inflating the balloons to coordinating their launch. As they gracefully rise into the air, these colorful and unique hot air balloons captivate all who are watching. They rise and are sent in different directions, filling the sky with their beautiful designs and vibrant colors. They are awe-inspiring for all who are watching.

Just like the magnificent balloons, each one of us is sent. We are sent to hospitals and schools, corporate offices and retail stores, restaurants and coffee shops, churches and non-profits, consulting firms and construction sites, bus depots and fire stations, airports and hotels—the list goes on and on. As we go, we are called to follow the leading of the Holy Spirit to bear witness to God through our lives and wisely share the Good News.

Let us pray for the Kingdom of God to come to our workplaces, our cities, our homes, and on earth as it is in heaven. This is our highest calling!

Tips and Biblical Encouragement

How can you share the Good News? Here are some tips:

1.   Remember that as Christians we can't be passive—being Great Commission people requires actions.

     He said to them, "Go into all the world and preach the gospel to all creation."

     — Mark 16:15

2.   Use wisdom when sharing the gospel. Share it as if someone's life depended on it—it does.

     Be wise in the way you act toward outsiders; make the most of every opportunity.

     — Colossians 4:5

3.   Being wise means it's Good News, not a weapon! This news comes through goodness and love, not judgment or coercion. God wants the world to be saved, not condemned.

*For God did not send his Son into the world to
condemn the world, but to save the world through
him.*

— John 3:17

4. God has put you in places to be a witness and a partner
    for reconciliation. Remember, this is your entire
    purpose in this world. God is depending on you.

    *How, then, can they call on the one they have not
    believed in? And how can they believe in the one of
    whom they have not heard? And how can they hear
    without someone preaching to them?*

    — Romans 10:14

5. Be proud of the gospel. Don't hide it under a bushel,
    but remember you are a shining example of the light in
    the darkness. Don't be ashamed of it but light up the
    world!

    *For I am not ashamed of the gospel, because it is the
    power of God that brings salvation to everyone who
    believes: first to the Jew, then to the Gentile.*

    — Romans 1:16

    *You are the light of the world. A town built on a hill
    cannot be hidden. Neither do people light a lamp and
    put it under a bowl. Instead they put it on its stand,
    and it gives light to everyone in the house. In the same*

way, let your light shine before others, that they may see your good deeds and glorify your Father in heaven.

— Matthew 5: 14–16

Reflective Questions

1. Isaiah 6:8 asks, "Whom shall I send?" How does your life reflect a readiness to respond, "Here am I. Send me!" in the context of living out the Great Commission?

2. Reflecting on the fruit of the Spirit (Galatians 5:22–23), which characteristic do you find most challenging to exhibit in your daily life, and how might growing in this area impact your ability to bear witness to others?

3. In what ways can you ensure that your actions and words genuinely reflect the love of Christ rather than causing others to view you through a lens of hypocrisy or judgment?

4. Consider the impact of evangelism rooted in fear versus evangelism rooted in love. How can you avoid using Scripture in a way that coerces or condemns and instead embody the love and grace of God?

5. How does your understanding of God's unconditional love shape your approach to sharing the Good News with others?

6. Reflect on Romans 10:14–15 and your personal role in the Great Commission. How can you be more

intentional in going out to share the Good News with those who have not heard it?

7.   Is your cubicle a sacred cubicle?

ACKNOWLEDGMENTS AND GRATITUDE

David: For twenty-nine years you have loved and supported me in anything I felt led, called, or simply wanted to do. Thank you for always being there, loving me, and letting me be me. (Even when it's crazy.) We have built quite an amazing life together. Thank you for reading *The Sacred Cubicle* and encouraging me throughout this process. I love you so much, pooky, and I can't wait to see what is next for us.

Sydney: You made me a mom! I am amazed by your talents. You have gifts that I could only dream of, and I pray you will use them to glorify the God of all creation. I adore you; I'd walk through fire for you; and I will love you till the end of time. I pray that as you continue to grow into adulthood, we continue to grow in our relationship as mother and daughter. I am so proud to call you my daughter!

Brooke: I love being your mom. You are the best travel partner ever, and I love all of our adventures. God has generously gifted you. You're like a firework stand on an old, dark highway, and you bring so much joy to those around you. I am so proud of the things you do for others and how you go out of your way to make people feel loved. You're amazing, just the way you are.

Laura: On 8/21/06 you walked into my office thinking you were going to get rid of me. That didn't quite go according to your plan. Kindness, goodness, and love radiate off you, and you are the single most gifted human I know. I am blessed by every single moment of our friendship. From the Kim & Laura Show, to Ms. Pacman, to bird watching in Eaton Canyon ILY22. Turns out you were right—it's all about the journey. I am so thankful that you and Ash are in my zip code.

Tara: I'll never forget on 5/22/16 seeing a woman preach for the first time. Wow. The Spirit worked through your preaching and teaching to transform my faith through curiosity and wonder. You encouraged me to use my gifts for the church and inspired me to write. I love being your ministry sidekick, Friday friend date, and personal Olivia Pope. I can't imagine my life if you hadn't first been my pastor and then my friend. I love you, and I am so grateful for you and Jeff.

Mom and Dad: The foundation of my life was set from the very beginning. Growing up in a loving home with a family I love and care for so much was pivotal to every step I have taken. Many of the experiences you gave me I have wanted to duplicate in my family. From the love of the national parks to the beach to Disney. The sacrifices you made for all of us were not taken for granted: Disneyland every year on my birthday, vacations, private schooling, and spontaneous trips. I guess I am living that one out to the extreme. Mom, thank you for always watching the kids and freeing me up to grow my career. They were so lucky to have you and grow up right beside their Krueger cousins. I love you so much, and there is nobody else I would want for my parents. Thank you for being the best parents and grandparents I could have ever imagined.

Becca: You were my very first friend in this world. As I was writing this, I paused and really reflected on our lives. From early on, playing Emergency!, having our own Camilla trees, raising chickens at Mia's, and building epic camping clubhouses—these are memories that are so easy to forget but such a gift to remember. To later, dressing as twins in high school, then getting married, living next to each other, and eventually having #thomger5. Thank you for years of praying for me. I love you.

Matt: Thanks for introducing me to Snoop Dogg and 90s rap. I loved growing up with you; you were with us for most of the memories I listed above. It was a pretty amazing childhood, and watching you grow up and use your gifts has been a joy. You are an example of kindness to others on and off the field. Love you and your family so much!

Rachel: You are the first sibling I remember being born. I was so excited to get to hold you in the hospital. One of my favorite memories with you was watching NBC movies of the week. Crime, drama, romance, and horrible acting, but we were there for it and thought they were amazing. I love laughing with you; one of the best laughs of my life was that night in Paris. Gosh, I wish I could remember what was so funny.

Corporate Andrew: As you know, I consider it an amazing privilege being able to work with you for nine years, and I hope we will work together again. We have become so much closer and I am so proud of you! Also, thank you for keeping me humble; if it weren't for you, I might have developed too big of an ego. I love you. Remind me, how do you like your In-N-Out Burgers?

James: You were born when I was seventeen. The chances of us being close were pretty slim, and yet we developed such a bond. When you were little, everyone thought you were my son—not that there's anything wrong with that. My favorite times with you are vacations, whether it's investigating rangers at the Canyon Campground, watching the wind slam doors in Many Glaciers, or ziplining in Puerto Vallarta. You are an amazing brother, and I will always stand by you. I am so proud to be your sister. I love you.

THOMGER5: I think the happiest period of my life was when you were all so little. Amma, your mom/aunt, and I had so much fun with you. Watching you all grow is crazy! Missions were awesome! Disneyland trips were so fun! Starbucks dates, swimming in Thomas Cove, and we can't forget our trip to Walt Disney World! Our annual girls plus one trip to Yellowstone is my favorite week of the year. I love you all so much, and I pray that each of you live a life of faithfulness, following Jesus, and bearing witness to our very good God.

TEACH: From early Disney days, to mundane moments, to ice cream shops, and epic vacations, it is such a joy doing life with you. Rest assured, there is no group I would rather make eight sandwiches for. I pray when we say, "Love the Lord your God with all of your heart, with all of your soul, with all of your mind and with all of your strength and love your neighbor as yourself," it's not just words but that we embody that with our lives. I love you and look forward to many more adventures.

Kim's Collection: You are the people that I bare my soul with. Each of you divinely entered my life at different stages. Each of you have been my champions and are gifts to me from God. Most of my profound conversations have occurred with each of you. In laughter and tears. Through marriages and divorces. Through new jobs and layoffs. In life and in death.

Same time zone or not. You have had a significant impact on my life. I love you, and I am blessed beyond measure by your friendship.

EUS Leaders: Thank you for leading alongside me. I want to thank each of you personally, but am so nervous I'll accidentally leave someone out. Whether you were leading through influence as an individual contributor or were in a formal leadership role, it was you working beside me to make EUS exactly what it was. Thank you for everything you did for me, our people, and our patients. You made our environment a Sacred Cubicle, and for that I am eternally grateful.

To my previous leaders: I have learned something from every single one of you! Many of you invested in me in big ways, and I am so appreciative for your time, advocacy, and lessons you imparted along the way. Thank you all! Michael Ann Huitron, DeeDee Cantu, Barbara Yankowski, Frank Vargas, Sharon Correa (best mentor), Rod Malone, Bob Redden, Sue Ludwig, Ray Moss, Mark Eimer, Dan Ulichnie, David Crofford, Phil Kelly, Mickey Davis, Joe Favazza, Jerry Hill, Joe Pastorelli, Brad Stewart, Michelle Weston, Ash Shehata, Richard Cortez, John Lough, Kristie Gobeli, Steve Bradbury, Deanna Wise, Dwayne Paul, Stan Martin, Randall Ganaway, and Leah Miller.

Barbara Yankowski, thank you for hiring me into healthcare. You called me as a twenty-year-old and offered me a job. I will never forget it.

Frank Vargas, you gave me a chance in information technology and an opportunity to grow. You had the foresight to ensure that in a male-dominated field, I had a woman mentor. Thank you.

Rod Malone, you promoted me to my first formal leadership role, and you were a model for me during my entire tenure in IT at CommonSpirit. I am grateful for your endless wisdom, humility, and friendship. It was an honor to serve beside you for as long as I did.

Ash, Ray, Dwayne, and **Stan,** I learned countless things from you throughout my career and life. Thank you for your mentorship, candor, and friendship.

To all those who contributed to my manuscript by submitting stories, reading, and providing feedback and endorsements: I thank you for your time and wisdom. I am so appreciative. This book would not have been possible without your engagement and support.

Christine Caine: Thank you for being so generous with your time. I have watched you as you embolden others for the Kingdom of God, and I am truly in awe of your generosity. Thank you for including me in Propel Women!

Faith: Without a doubt, you have been the biggest encourager of *The Sacred Cubicle*. I likely wouldn't have completed it without your constant encouragement, and you gave it its name.

Larry: I couldn't imagine my life if I hadn't met you more than twenty-five years ago. Since I was a baby leader, you have been by my side, faithfully and tirelessly. The work you did gave me time and emboldened me to do what I did for others. Always humbly behind the scenes, you were the brains behind so much of my career success. Thank you, I am so grateful.

ENDNOTES

Introduction

1 Goldin, Kara. 2019. "5 Ways to Demonstrate Integrity at Work Today." *Forbes*, February 26, 2019. https://www.forbes.com/sites/karagoldin/2019/02/26/five-ways-to-demonstrate-your-integrity-at-work/.

2 Keller, Timothy. *Every Good Endeavor: Connecting Your Work to God's Work*. New York: Dutton, 2012, 20.

3 Villodas, Rich. *The Deeply Formed Life: Five Transformative Values to Root Us in the Way of Jesus*. Colorado Springs, CO: WaterBrook, 2020, 206.

4 Barna Group, *Christians at Work: Examining Vocational Calling and Faith at Work in America* (Ventura, CA: Barna Group, 2018).

5 Workship. "Faith and Work Integration." *Workship*, August 21, 2019. Accessed August 26, 2022. https://www.workship.com.au/blog/21/8/2019/faith-and-work-integration.

Chapter 1: Joy

6   Teresa, Mother Saint. 1987. *Love, a Fruit Always in Season Daily Meditations from the Words of Mother Teresa of Calcutta*. San Francisco Ignatius Press. 94.

7   Liu, Alex, Beth Bovis, and Kim Fulton. "To Have Joy in the Workplace, There Must Be Justice for All." *MIT Sloan Management Review*, June 17, 2022. https://sloan-review.mit.edu/article/to-have-joy-in-the-workplace-there-must-be-justice-for-all/.

8   Merriam-Webster.com Dictionary. "Joy." Accessed August 19, 2022. https://www.merriam-webster.com/dictionary/joy.

9   Liu, Alex. *Joy Works: Empowering Teams in the New Era of Work*. Hoboken, NJ: Wiley, 2022.

10   Markway, Barbara. "15 Habits That Will Grow Your Happiness." *Psychology Today*, October 28, 2013. Accessed April 21, 2022. https://www.psychologytoday.com/us/blog/shyness-is-nice/201310/15-habits-will-grow-your-happiness.

11   Belli, Gina. "Here's How Many Years You'll Spend at Work in Your Lifetime." *Fairygodboss*, October 1, 2018. Accessed June 22, 2023. https://fairygodboss.com/career-topics/heres-how-many-years-youll-spend-at-work-in-your-lifetime.

Chapter 2: Peace

12 Henri Nouwen. 2005. *Peacework: Prayer, Resistance, Community*. Orbis Books.

13 Rench, Larry, email message to author, February 2, 2023.

14 Morse, MaryKate. *A Guidebook to Prayer: Twenty-Four Ways to Walk with God*. Downers Grove, IL: IVP Books, 2013, 131. Accessed October 21, 2020. https://books.apple.com/id818873556.

15 *Exhale Prayer*. Hosted by Faith Romasco and Jason Marsh, 2017–present.

16 Cowman, L. B. *Streams in the Desert*. Updated edition. Grand Rapids, MI: Zondervan, 1997.

Chapter 3: Patience

17 Vreeland, Derek. 2019. *By the Way: Getting Serious about Following Jesus*. Herald Press.

18 Power, Rhett. 2017. "4 Tips to Help You Be a More Patient Person, Science Says You Will Be Happier." Inc.com. Inc. October 24, 2017. https://www.inc.com/rhett-power/4-tips-to-help-you-be-a-more-patient-person-science-says-you-will-be-happier.html.

19 Cleveland Clinic. "How To Be Patient: 6 Strategies to Help You Keep Your Cool." *Health Essentials*, June

5, 2024. Accessed November 24, 2024. https://health.clevelandclinic.org/how-to-be-patient.

20   DiGiulio, Sarah. "Here's How to Curb Your Impatience Once and for All, and Finally Feel Less Stressed." *Big Think*, July 21, 2019. Accessed October 17, 2023. https://www.nbcnews.com/better/lifestyle/how-train-yourself-be-more-patient-ncna1022356

21   Spiegel, James S. *How to Be Good in a World Gone Bad: Living a Life of Christian Virtue.* Grand Rapids, MI: Kregel Publications, 2004.

22   Wright, Christopher J.H. *Cultivating the Fruit of the Spirit: Growing in Christlikeness.* Downers Grove, IL: IVP Books, 2017.

23   Blevins, Dean G., and Mark A. Maddix. *Discovering Discipleship: Dynamics of Christian Education.* Kansas City, MO: Beacon Hill Press, 2010.

24   Warren, Tish Harrison. *Liturgy of the Ordinary: Sacred Practices in Everyday Life.* Downers Grove, IL: InterVarsity Press, 2016.

Chapter 4: Kindness

25   Christian Nestell Bovee. 1857. *Thoughts, Feelings, and Fancies.* 109.

26   Cooke, Rachel. "Never Trust Anyone Who Is Rude to a Waiter." *The Guardian.* Accessed February 23,

2022. https://www.theguardian.com/lifeandstyle/2013/jun/15/never-trust-anyone-rude-waiter.

27   Dean, Lloyd. "The Power of Compassion to Drive Your Bottom Line." *Center for Compassion and Altruism Research and Education*, March 19, 2014. Accessed October 26, 2024. https://ccare.stanford.edu/press_posts/the-power-of-compassion-to-drive-your-bottom-line/.

28   Global Leadership Network. "Behind TOMS Founder Blake Mycoskie's Plan to Build an Army of Social Entrepreneurs." *Global Leadership Network*, Accessed January 5, 2024. https://globalleadership.org/articles/leading-organizations/behind-toms-founder-blake-mycoskies-plan-build-army-social-entrepreneurs/.

29   Sezer, Ovul, Kelly Nault, and Nadav Klein. "Don't Underestimate the Power of Kindness at Work." *Harvard Business Review*, May 7, 2021. Accessed June 20, 2022. https://hbr.org.

30   Brown, Brené. *Dare to Lead: Brave Work. Tough Conversations. Whole Hearts.* New York: Random House, 2018.

31   McClain, Lisa, email message to author, October 2, 2022

Chapter 5: Goodness

32   Frank, Anne. 2008. *Anne Frank's Tales from the Secret Annex*. Bantam, 120.

33   *Dictionary.com.* "Goodness." Accessed May 18, 2023.
      https://www.dictionary.com/browse/goodness.

34   Wright, Christopher J.H. *Cultivating the Fruit of the
      Spirit: Growing in Christlikeness.* Downers Grove, IL:
      IVP Books, 2017, 98.

35   Ibid.

36   Ibid., 100.

37   Ibid., 53.

38   Packer, J.I. *Reflected Glory. Christianity Today,*
      December 2003. Accessed January 25, 2024. https://
      www.christianitytoday.com/2003/12/reflected-glory/.

39   Rohr, Richard. *The Universal Christ: How a Forgotten
      Reality Can Change Everything We See, Hope For, and
      Believe.* New York: Convergent Books, 2019, 59-61.

40   Rohr, Richard. *The Universal Christ: How a Forgotten
      Reality Can Change Everything We See, Hope For, and
      Believe.* New York: Convergent Books, 2019, 61–63.

41   Graham, Billy. "How Can I Ever Be Good Enough
      for God?" *Billy Graham Evangelistic Association.*
      Accessed July 25, 2023. https://billygraham.org/answer/
      how-can-i-ever-be-good-enough-for-god/.

42   Rohr, Richard. "The Shadow of Original Sin." *Center for
      Action and Contemplation*, October 25, 2021. Accessed
      May 9, 2023. https://cac.org/daily-meditations/
      the-shadow-of-original-sin-2021-10-25/.

43   Relevant Magazine. "Fighting for Good in a World That Isn't." *Relevant Magazine*, May 19, 2023 2024. Accessed October, 4, 2023. https://relevantmagazine.com/faith/fighting-for-good-in-a-world-that-isnt/.

44   Perna, Mark. "5 Marks of a Toxic Work Culture—And How You Know It's Time to Leave." *Forbes*, June 13, 2023. Accessed December 22, 2023. https://markcperna.com/5-marks-of-a-toxic-work-culture-and-how-you-know-its-time-to-leave/.

45   Molano, Sarah. "These Are the Signs That You're in a Toxic Work Environment." *CNN*, July 20, 2022. Accessed February 26, 2024. https://www.cnn.com/2022/07/20/health/toxic-workplace-signs-solutions-wellness/index.html.

46   Stillman, Jessica. "Adam Grant to Job Seekers and Business Leaders: Beware the 4Rs of Toxic Workplace Culture." *Inc.*, August 21, 2023. Accessed January 23, 2024. https://www.inc.com/jessica-stillman/adam-grant-wharton-toxic-workplaces.html.

47   Impicciche, Joseph R. "In Support of Justice and Peace." *About Ascension*, May 30, 2020. Accessed September 22, 2023. https://about.ascension.org/news/2020/05/in-support-of-justice-and-peace.

48   Vreeland, Derek. *By the Way: Getting Serious about Following Jesus*. Harrisonburg, VA: Herald Press, 2022.

49   Palmer, Sean. *Unarmed Empire: In Search of Beloved Community*. Eugene, OR: Cascade Books, 2017.

Accessed through Apple Books. https://books.apple.com/us/book/unarmed-empire/id1453303988.

50   Ely, Robin J., and David A. Thomas. "Getting Serious About Diversity: Enough Already with the Business Case." *Harvard Business Review* 98, no. 6 (November–December 2020): 114–122.

51   Villodas, Rich. *The Deeply Formed Life: Five Transformative Values to Root Us in the Way of Jesus.* Colorado Springs, CO: WaterBrook, 2020, 82-83.

Chapter 6: Gentleness

52   Lucado, Max. 2016. "It's a New Day: The Choice Is Yours - Max Lucado." Max Lucado. May 25, 2016. https://maxlucado.com/new-day-choice/.

53   Cambridge Dictionary. "Gentle." Accessed November 2, 2023. https://dictionary.cambridge.org/dictionary/english/gentle.

54   Wright, Christopher. *Cultivating the Fruit of the Spirit: Growing in Christlikeness.* Downers Grove, IL: IVP Books, 2017, 67.

55   Wilson, Gerald H. *Psalms Volume 1: The NIV Application Commentary.* Grand Rapids, MI: Zondervan, 2002, 145.

56   Dickerson, Matthew. "The Counter-Cultural Virtues of Gentleness and Kindness." *De Pree Center.* Accessed February 21, 2024. https://depree.org/

the-counter-cultural-virtues-of-gentleness-and-kind-ness.

57   Aquinas, Thomas. *Summa Theologica*, II-II, Q. 157.

58   McKnight, Scot. *Sermon on the Mount*. Grand Rapids, MI: Zondervan, 2013, 42.

59   Stott, John. *The Beatitudes: Developing Spiritual Character*. Downers Grove, IL: IVP, 1998, 25.

60   Wesley, John. *Sermon 22: Upon Our Lord's Sermon on the Mount, Discourse II*. In *The Works of John Wesley*, Vol. 1. Nashville, TN: Abingdon Press, 1984, 489–490.

Chapter 7: Self-Control

61   Ziglar, Zig. 2007. *Ziglar on Selling: The Ultimate Handbook for the Complete Sales Professional*. Thomas Nelson.

62   Karnesky, Dustin email message to author, May 2, 2024

63   Ibid.

64   Faust, James E. "Honesty—a Moral Compass." *The Friend*, November 2001. Accessed April 7, 2023. https://www.churchofjesuschrist.org/study/friend/2001/11/come-listen-to-a-prophets-voice-honesty-a-moral-compass?lang=eng.

65   Nangle, Joshua. "Self-Control in the Workplace." *Institute for Faith, Work & Economics*, February 21,

2022. Accessed April 17, 2023. https://tifwe.org/
self-control-in-the-workplace.

Chapter 8: Faithfulness

66   Caine, Christine. Twitter post. February 26, 2020.
Accessed March 27, 2023. https://x.com/christinecaine/
status/1232847854525407238.

67   Jethani, Skye. *What If Jesus Was Serious?: A Visual Guide
to the Teachings of Jesus We Love to Ignore*. Chicago:
Moody Publishers, 2020.

68   Vreeland, Derek. *By the Way: Getting Serious about Following Jesus*. Harrisonburg, VA: Herald Press, 2019, 89.
Accessed January 20, 2023. https://books.apple.com/us/
book/by-the-way/id1452644907.

69   Leach, Tara Beth. *Kingdom Culture: The Sermon on the
Mount*. The Foundry Publishing, 2020.

Chapter 9: Love

70   King, Martin Luther, Jr. "Loving Your Enemies."
Sermon, Dexter Avenue Baptist Church, Montgomery,
AL, November 17, 1957. Accessed January 5, 2024.
https://kinginstitute.stanford.edu/king-papers/doc-
uments/loving-your-enemies-sermon-delivered-dex-
ter-avenue-baptist-church.

71   "Author Talks: How to Fall in Love with
Work." *McKinsey & Company*, Accessed

June 22, 2024. https://www.mckinsey.
com/featured-insights/mckinsey-on-books/
author-talks-how-to-fall-in-love-with-work.

72   Hagan, Ekua. "What's Love Got to Do with Work?"
Psychology Today, February 11, 2022. Accessed June 15,
2024. https://www.psychologytoday.com/intl/blog/
are-you-aware/202202/whats-love-got-do-work.

73   King, Levi. "9 Ways to Show Your Employees You
Love Them." *Inc.*, February 14, 2018. Accessed June 15,
2024. https://www.inc.com/levi-king/9-ways-to-show-
your-employees-you-love-them.html.

74   Chapter 10: Living the Great Commission Choung,
James. 2022. *True Story Bible Study*. InterVarsity Press.

75   Leach, Tara Beth. *Radiant Church: Restoring the Credibility of Our Witness*. Downers Grove, IL: IVP, 2021,
141-142.

76   Villodas, Rich. *The Deeply Formed Life: Five Transformative Values to Root Us in the Way of Jesus*. Colorado
Springs, CO: WaterBrook, 2020, 212.

77   Villodas, Rich. *The Deeply Formed Life: Five Transformative Values to Root Us in the Way of Jesus*. Colorado
Springs, CO: WaterBrook, 2020, 213.

78   "Balloon Fiesta Set an All-Time Attendance Record
in 2023." *KOB 4*, October 19, 2023. Accessed May 28,
2024. https://www.kob.com/new-mexico/balloon-fies-
ta-set-an-all-time-attendance-record-in-2023/.

www.ingramcontent.com/pod-product-compliance
Lightning Source LLC
LaVergne TN
LVHW012244140225
803765LV00003B/3

9 7 9 8 8 9 5 9 7 2 4 2 7